OURSTORY...

Indian Response To Nineteenth Century Literature

THE purpose of this collection, diverse with respect to issues, genres and forms, is to insert literary writing in a larger historical framework. Literature is important not merely in itself but as an activity that takes place in a concrete and dynamic context. *"Role"* and *"function"* would be big words. Nonetheless, certain writers belong to a special category of individuals who manifest in their endeavour a sensitivity and r e s p o n s i v e n e s s to their world.

So far, literary scholars in India have carried the academicist bias. It is a value-neutral, *"objective"* bias according to which any and every approach, from retrogressive to the most *"radical"*, would be good enough for projection. However, living as we do in a context which is culturally distanced from countries in the West, our standpoint has to be specific and distinct — it has to be *"positional"*. The authors and texts we have read for about a century give us signals other than they give to the western reader. It is only appropriate that we not only recognize but also interpret and assess them.

The study of English and other western literatures in relation to our own bears consideration on two counts. Firstly, it is a compliment to the unceasing vitality and dynamism of those works which should have been integrally connected with our own human and social concerns. Secondly, it points towards the *"waste of energy"* that takes place in our academia where we fail to make them a part of **OURSTORY**. Emerging from a complex mingling of historical forces, the study of English literature in India should be representative of the reality, both theirs and ours, existing at the time. The *"universality"* of literature gets redefined in its ability to speak different languages to different peoples.

Ourstory - II
Critical Theory in the Third World

The last few decades have manifested an increasing tendency in literature and thought to turn inwards and examine the very roots on which these stood. It is not merely the psychology, the mental make-up, the workings of consciousness of men and women as individuals but the psychologies hidden behind philolosophical concepts, verbal constructs, specific responses, popular perceptions that have come to occupy centre of attention today. The "meaning of meaning" is an old phrase in comparison to the "theory of theory" and "practice of theory." Likewise, language as an autonomous entity is stretched to the utmost so that we gain entry into the origins of knowledge. Sometimes, we do get shocked to hear that the same language proves to be a cruel mistress and makes prisoners of us all. However, our intellectual-theoretical environment is not all that maddening. Tangible patterns emerge whenever there is a clash of vested philosophical and other interests. All variations, disagreements, multiplicities, pluralities, etc. vanish when actual pressures start working upon power-centres. During such periods, we notice clear perspectives along lines of weak and strong parts of the world. Critical theory strikes firm roots through its positioning in the interests of the exploited and underprivileged.

This volume on critical theory proposes to offer analysis and critique of important developments in areas related to the interpretation and understanding of literature. Our perspective continues to be the centredness we have in our own socio-cultural surroundings from where all literatures — European, American, African, Latin American, Indian — make sense to us as situated in a third world country aware of a need for dignity and equality with the rest of the people in the world.

Aspects we intend to cover are :
* Dominant Structures and Literature
* Text and Context : Re-Interpreting Literature
* Study of Literature : Market-Friendly or Knowledge-Based ?
* Historicising Literary Theories
* Genre and Form : Limitations of Theoretical Frameworks
* Feminist Responses : Limitations and Potential

— **M.L., S.K. & A.P. (Eds.)**

Ourstory - III
Theory and Practice of Translation

Editors : Mohua Lahiri, Sanjay Kumar and Anand Prakash

Ourstory...

Indian Response to Nineteenth Century Literature

Editors

Mohua Lahiri
Sanjay Kumar
Anand Prakash

Academic Foundation
DELHI

Published : 1992 by
Academic Foundation
24 - A, Sriram Road, Civil Lines, Delhi - 110 054. (INDIA).
Phone : 232966, 2911852 & 233730.

Copyright : Academic Foundation.
© 1992 [AF]

ALL RIGHTS RESERVED.
No part of this work may be reproduced or utilized for trade purposes, in any form or by any means, electronic or mechanical, including photocopying, recording, or by any information storage and retrieval system, without permission in writing from the publisher.

OURSTORY :

INDIAN RESPONSE TO NINETEENTH CENTURY LITERATURE
Edited by Mohua Lahiri, Sanjay Kumar and Anand Prakash

ISBN-81-7188-088-6

Designed, Laser-typeset & Printed by :
COMPRINT INDIA
Delhi - 110054

Contents...

1. **Introduction** 9

2. **Learning & Teaching
   — Keats' *Odes* :**
   P.K. Dutta 25

3. **The Idea of Poverty
   in the Novels of Dickens**
   Sambudha Sen 41

4. **F.R. Leavis on *Hard Times***
   O.P. Grewal 63

5. **'The Wings of the Dove
   "not knowing, but only guessing"'**
   Kumkum Sangari 77

6. **Writing in Ourselves**
   Zakia Pathak 95

7. **Fiction or Historical Positioning? :
   — A Reading of J.G. Farrell's
   *The Siege of Krishnapur***
   Sanjay Kumar 111

8. **Of Indian History and
   English Studies**
   A Discussion with
   Bipan Chandra 125

INDEX 156

The Contributors

Bipan Chandra : Professor of History in the School of Social Sciences, J.N.U. His doctoral dissertation was on *The Rise of Economic Nationalism in India*, which later came out in book form. He has written extensively on contemporary political and ideological problems including communalism on which he has a full-length study.

Kumkum Sangari : Teaches English at I.P. College, Delhi. She got her Ph.D. on James and Fitzgerald. She has published extensively on American literature, English literature, Latin American literature and *Sati*.

O.P. Grewal : Professor in the Department of English, Kurukshetra University, Kurukshetra. His Ph.D. dissertation on Henry James has been published under the title *Henry James and the Ideology of Culture*. Subjects on which he has written include Georg Lukacs, New Criticism, Kamala Das, Muktibodh and Contemporary Hindi Poetry.

P.K. Dutta : Teaches English at Sri Venkateswara College in Delhi University and is doing his Ph.D. on "Communalism in Bengal : 1923-1930." He has published articles on communalism and Indian Writing in English.

Sambudha Sen : Teaches English at Sri Venkateswara College in Delhi University and has completed his Ph.D. on Charles Dickens. He has published articles on Tolstoy and Communalism in India.

Zakia Pathak : Taught English at Miranda House, Delhi till July 1991. She has published articles on Shah Bano and Margaret Drabble.

Editors

Mohua Lahiri (M.Phil., Ll.B.) : Currently editing school work-books for Ryan Publishers and Distributors, Pvt. Ltd. She taught English at various colleges in Delhi University.

Sanjay Kumar (M.Phil.) : Teaches English at Hans Raj College, Delhi. He is actively involved in Student Theatre dealing with third world issues.

Anand Prakash (Ph.D.) : Teaches English at Hans Raj College, Delhi. He has published extensively on trends in Contemporary Hindi fiction and has translated short stories, poems and theoretical works. His doctoral dissertation is to be shortly published under the title *Marxism and Literary Theory*.

1

Introduction

The study as well as teaching of English Literature in Indian Universities as opposed to its reading has for some time been the cause of heated exchanges. The blurring of boundaries between English Literature and English Language teaching has further served to make the issue complex. The introduction of English in India was due to a multiplicity of historical and imperialistic concerns when the presence of the English here underwent several changes from being a primarily trading activity to a desire for administrative dominance. But more than four decades after the British have left India, English studies continue to form a part of the curriculum of the major Universities. Raymond Williams in his *Marxism and Literature* talked extensively of how the shifting of the economic base does not necessarily lead to a corresponding shift in the superstructure. Residual formations owing their origins to past historical formations very often continue into a new era, but are then subjected to pressures resulting from a shift in power equations.

A major questioning of the study of English comes from the questioning of the humanistic education model itself. The sharp shift towards a more utilitarian scheme well articulated by the New Education Policy of 1986, articulates in precise terms the existing trend where the best students invariably opt for applied Science Courses like Engineering and Medicine and others opt for Commerce or Economics which give them a better chance for M.B.A. Courses. The question often asked is, what do you do after studying English ? Today even journalism which earlier welcomed English students often requires specialisation in fields like economics, politics etc., and so the English student is left behind in the competition. To that extent the "Crisis of English Studies" is a global phenomenon and finds its echo in the Indian Universities, too. The difference is that with us there is an added dimension to what constitutes Literature because of an emerging voice that insists that Indian writing in English should constitute a dominant part of the syllabus. But, even in careers which still remain open to English students, like advertising or journalism, the emphasis is really on language proficiency and modern usages and the syllabus content of English does not go beyond literature of the nineteen forties. So the student's knowledge of the language comes really from extensive reading and exposure to books, films and music which find no representation in the syllabus.

The questioning of English teaching, however, does not come only from utilitraian concerns. A serious attack is mounted by people who question the continuance of English as the National Language and the use of the two language formula. Though Hindi is the second National Language, yet more and more students' voices have been heard demanding the removal of English as the other National Language. The attack is on two counts. Firstly, English as the language of the erstwhile rulers is a representation of the colonial yoke. Secondly, and more importantly, English is the language of the elite, therefore a small minority, and so does not represent the larger mass of people whereas Hindi is spoken in a number of states and is understood by a larger majority of people. But, both the arguments point towards a perceptible shift in the power equations between the various classes of people as also the dominant role that the five states of Uttar Pradesh, Bihar, Rajasthan, Madhya Pradesh, and Haryana play in national politics.

The counter argument has been that the imposition of Hindi on non-Hindi speaking states may give rise to more problems. Thus, it is ironical that the colonizers today take the credit for creating the geopolitical India of today as well as providing a language which precisely because it does not represent any one region also serves as the link language. This is not, however, to ignore the fact that English also is the language of the elite classes of the professionals and to some extent the bureaucrats.

The opposition to the teaching of English, however, slides over the difference between the teaching of the Language and the teaching of Literature. The reasons cited for opposition to the study of the Language, however, do not necessarily coincide with the hostility to the study of English literature. In an ironic reversal of the moralistic underpinnings of orientalist studies, the study of English and Western literature on the whole is also seen as an exposure to the depraved and immoral social codes of western societies. The study of English literature somehow corrupts the innocent mind and the sobriquet "westernised" is often used as an insult in social discourse just as to be westernised is also to be non-Indian in one's identity and therefore, anti-national.

The third critique against English studies is in some ways an extension of the above argument. It is now a more or less accepted academic approach to relocate a literary text in its historical space. But what historical space are we alluding to ? The text in its moment of inception or at its moment of reception ? The students or teachers of English studies in India have to counter the criticism about their concern for social conditions of a distant land whereas the social reality in which they are immersed is far removed from them. The teaching of English cannot afford to remain aloof from its own historical realities.

To some degree the process has already begun with many teachers in various universities branching off in their research into various areas. Three major areas of possible research have emerged in the past few years which could open the scope of English studies in India to make it more relevant to its own social realities. It is in this interaction with western thought and their literature, where they serve as catalysts as well as critiques of more indigenous perspectives, that English Studies can move out of its colonial origin.

The Sahitya Akademi has for sometime been actively sponsoring the translation of literature in Indian languages to other languages. In fact, translation studies remains a most dynamic area for research, keeping in mind the already rich collection of Indian literary texts that exist with many Indians being genuinely bi-lingual if not multi-lingual. It opens up the vast area of not only dealing with perceptions of Indian reality but also how different languages and cultures negotiate between reality and its perception. The second area is the study of English literature within the whole colonial framework. In fact, the interpretation of colonial discourse has been one of the most stimulating debates that has been going on in the Indian universities, especially in the interaction between the English and History Departments.

The third possible area of research is in the comparative study of the Indian Aesthetic Theories and their Western counterparts. India has a long history of influences that have contributed towards creating a very rich cultural heritage. Many of its art forms have a very evolved theoretical framework and it would make a very interesting area of research to see whether these cultural formations unconsciously and indirectly intervene in the reading of western texts. Here the classroom dynamics in the university often provide a rather fecund ground for such explorations and in fact many lecturers have been focussing their attention on precisely this area of research.

What becomes crucial is the study of English literature in India, not just the "beginnings" but the continuation of it even though the political bearings of the teachers and students have undergone a sea change. Western criticism, including the intellectually stimulating critical theories, continues to dominate what can be called the Academic scene. By "Academic" is meant the formal acceptance which in several ways influences the setting of the syllabus and the framing of examination questions. Very often a parallel teaching method is followed where teachers teach what excites them and students lap it up but adhere to the status-quo when answering questions in the examinations. Why ?

At the root of this book is a desire to examine this question. We would like to understand the analysis and insights teachers and students have which they think should be censored from academic discussions. To do that, it may be useful to look at Delhi University in the last three decades to understand what have been the accepted norms and standards for the teaching of English literature in the University.

Delhi University has a hierarchical structure. The Undergraduate Courses are taught at various Colleges which offer Honours Courses or Pass Courses, Honours meaning specialisation in that particular subject. Postgraduate classes are more centralised and are taught at the North and South campuses by Readers and Professors and a handful of college teachers who are invited to do some texts. The tutorials are held in the colleges. The M.Phil Courses are exclusively conducted by Readers and Professors in the Department who form the University Faculty. The system ensures that the University Department remains totally cut off from the actual teaching that takes place in the undergraduate classes but retains the authority to conduct the examinations and structure the syllabi.

It is not necessary to state that the teaching in the undergraduate classes must function in the limited space that exists after taking into consideration the syllabi framed and the trend of questions in the examinations. The teaching experience of the University Department is vastly different from that of the English faculty in the colleges.

The teaching of English at the undergraduate level is itself a very peculiar though meaningful exercise. The marked difference between the Honours (the more privileged course) students and the Pass (which carries on the tradition of language and literature divide) students, the difference in the areas and objectives of the students who take these courses, as well as the difference in the familiarity with the language and literature between students going to the various colleges makes teaching at the undergraduate level a particular an extremely significant experience.

This experience is not necessarily shared by the University Department who teach mainly those students who opt for an academic line. If we accept that meaning is continually defined through its contexts, then the meaning of literature takes on different sets of meanings for the University Department and the College teachers.

What does the study of English literature mean to us in India? How and to what extent is it relevant to us? Certainly, our needs are not those of the students of literature in the West. We are not greatly interested in learning Anglo-Catholic ways of confronting our world, a waste land where nothing grows. Nor can we be deeply involved as common Indians with the fate of a mythic young boy, representing the process of development of the essential human character. This process of growing up is shown in a modern text in which the boy hates his father and moves closer to his mother, herself a victim of many excesses committed by an insensitive male. We do not deny the greatness of Eliot as a poet and the profundity of Lawrence as a novelist and thinker, the two modern writers we have in mind. Our contention is that these writers appeal to only those among us who belong to the upper middle class and share the frustrations, vacuities and shallownesses of that class. We have to constantly remind ourselves that our upper middle class is cut off from the larger mainstream constituting the toiling and suffering humanity. The important question is not of a barren land but of a barren system that ignores the toiling people's basic needs of bread, shelter, clothing and education. Eliot and Lawrence and others belonging to the same category are no doubt authentic products of their particular sociocultural environment; to that extent they strike a chord of sympathy among western audiences. They make the readers aware of the complexities of what is called "the human condition," a phrase loaded with many ideological meanings. Their preferences for a past distant from the modern men and women notwithstanding, they tell the people situated near them geographically and socially quite a few things that need to be pondered over, analysed, understood and shared. But to us they largely symbolise a way of life under which most concerns are ahistorical and metaphysical, or at least tenuously linked with our lives. The modernity of these English writers is of a piece with things that appear to most of us as historically unrealizable. Of course, we can place them in the context of a larger unified world in which the unity has been forged, through imposition, between a part which contains affluence and privileges and the other which is compelled to live in conditions of abject poverty. The two parts are organically linked, the latter allowing the fruits of its labour to be taken away by the former part so that the western capitalist world is sustained.

It is interesting that most of the twentieth century English writers offer negative examples of creativity, victims as they seem to us of a system that has turned them into "pathological" entities — it is a different matter though that unto themselves they are great visionaries, rebels, saints, etc. The reason why they are not happy with their surroundings and have no sense of belonging compels them to look towards an early past that kept man in a state of naturalness and innocence. One can also see in them the desire to retrieve a mythological world which, in their view, contains possibilities of meaning for man today.

Under the perspective of relevance and usefulness, we can counter the modernist western trend in literature in two distinct ways. One would be that we evolve through rigorous analysis of the trend an appropriate awareness of the nature of contemporary writing — the more knowledgeable we are about how particular literary works are shaped under contemporary pressures, the more able would we be to invent ways to work out questions related with them. Such an analysis would entail an attitude of recognising the objective entity of the modernist trend — the idea that it emerged under concrete conditions to fulfil a specific requirement. How broadly or adequately the requirement was fulfilled is something that again can be taken up if needed.

The second is that we examine our own cultural-ideological and social needs as a country and a community. The assumption, a valid one we hope, is that we do not need all that a trend emerging elsewhere would offer to us in our context. There is no doubt that having been a colony of British imperialism for close to two centuries, we have been drawn into the cultural vortex of western societies; as a result their idiom makes some sense and is intelligible to us to a large extent. But the same fact also makes us aware of our position as victims of the socio-political arrangement prevailing in the west. Once again, we have to make a distinction between conscious cultural strategies drawn by the imperialist power and those that reach us in a form, because of the same fact, different from the ones conceived by sensitive, humanist, even though conservative and conformist western writers. The context in such a case is so important that valuable and sympathetic perceptions change colour and become their very opposite. This has been quite effectively projected in E.M. Forster's *A Passage to India*.

The phrase "the third world" has caught on in the last few years in literature, particularly literary criticism. Serious scholars and thinkers even in the west realised the significance of a position from where European and other western literatures can be viewed critically. This position also involves the possibility, on the part of third world writers and critics, of creating an alternative paradigm of experience and thought. There is a whole lot of writing that makes sense to us in a different way, call it the recognition of inequality, exploitation, injustice or the struggle to achieve humanistic ideals. These can no longer be dubbed nineteenth century responses. In our view, these responses have not become irrelevant in the modern times of technological excellence and increasing complexities. For us from India, things are quite simple, and not embarrassingly. Strong prejudices deeply ingrained in the sensibilities of both the haves and have-nots in the western capitalist societies come to surface whenever the vested interests of the first world are threatened economically-militarily, or even held in question politically. These prejudices are gifts from modern imperialism and few western writers or thinkers, if at all, can escape them, except through a long and arduous intellectual struggle as well as through emotional involvement with the underprivileged and struggling in the third world societies. Names that come to mind are Sartre, Bertrand Russell, Graham Greene and a few more. And the quality of their writing, thought and behaviour, the values they evolved in the process are unique and greatly inspiring.

Why? A large number of middle class individuals even in the third world countries betray propensities that cut at the root of their broader social interests. That we have to raise the obvious question today speaks eloquently of the shrinking value-system we so gloriously developed in our days of nationalist struggle against British imperialism. To set things right, we have to evolve a different kind of humanism from the one which our nationalist writers projected through their writings, much as we value them. What we require is not an all-class humanism (liberal humanism of our time is one of the manifestations of it) since that makes us overlook the deadening impact of imperialism as well as the specific capitalisms of the third world countries, the two working almost all the time in unison. We require a humanism that is ruthlessly critical, uncompromising, dynamic and fearless. Our belief is that only such a humanism can deliver our toiling masses, though it is a long fight, from the clutches of multifaceted, multi-dimensional and extremely cynical imperialism.

Some of us English teachers discussed the nature of relationship between the Delhi University English Department and the English Departments in the University's constituent colleges. The university Department's chief concern was academic excellence, in a narrow esoteric way, in the field of literature. We saw behind this concern an assumption that the study of English literature would be better served through the production of MAs and MPhils. These are the two specialized literature courses offered by the University Department in which exclusive emphasis is laid on the study of literature.

"Literature," the word is problematic, generally stands for diversity in human and social experience expressed through the aesthetic mould. There would not be much quarrel with this but that it is too broad a definition. For instance, "human" could communicate that which happened to an individual human psyche at a given time, the layers of experience being revealed to the artist, a human being himself, who feels and experiences in the act of creation, and the myriad shades of common perceptions and responses found among people in society. The development of the artist into a representative sensibility occurs as a consequence of his absorbing the larger social experiences. To put it simply, the writer, being situated in the middle of such as environment effects, according to this thinking, a close identification with the people around him and expresses their emotions in his works. In this context, "human" implies that which binds all members of a community and society with a broader human entity and sees them as sharing common traits with one another. What emerges from this is the idea that there exist all-embracing conditions in society at a particular time and that they appear as determining agents, control as they do the social and intellectual behaviour of men and women in general. Human beings, according to such a thinking, are a homogeneous category more or less equally prone to social pressures, equally free or unfree. No contradiction is seen that could divide society into two mutually opposed, antagonistic groups. This is what we are taught to believe in and accept. Or at least this is assumed to be the case by those who conduct the study of literature in higher Departments, communicating more and more of the "human condition" and "the human predicament" to the students.

This explanation of the process of artistic production is individual-centred. It accords undue significance to the sensibility and personality of the writer engaged in the production of literature at different levels. The whole process of writing is seen by us as taking place in the writer's mind, which, when charged with creative energy, expresses the human experience in a crystallised form. The whole phraseology of the definition of the process is abstract. In the final analysis, it lays excessive emphasis on the creative-psychic energies of an individual human being. From an enigma, the artistic process under such a scheme grows into an entirely unknowable phenomenon. Mercifully, this perspective has weakened over the years, though we still have a number of diehards clinging to timelessness and perennialism in literature.

During the last few decades, we have also noticed in literary study a growing regard for society and history and the faculty of analysis, all of which could be covered under "social experience." This has resulted from social tensions generated by a host of factors. We know for certain that the India of the seventies and eighties is not the same as of the two decades preceding them. Many important economic and political changes have taken place in the mean time. While the upper middle class bias has lost its grip on the minds of the economically weaker intelligensia, another attitude has started emerging on the socio-cultural horizon. For instance, it appeared in the fifties and sixties that ideals of equality, justice and democratic living had struck roots in our society and were to stay for a long time. However, it proved to be an illusion as with subsequent years was unfolded the basic contradiction of bourgeois democracy—the antagonism between economic power and social rights of the citizens. Everyday, we witness the misuse of democratic processes by the privileged so that the rights of the underprivileged are negated. It happens at subtle as well as not-so-subtle levels, what with intellectuals and analysts trying to prove through argument that which the crude controllers and sharers of social power indulge in unabashedly. We ourselves become irrelevant to society we live in and are unable to communicate with fellow human beings.

However, there is a good side to this development. The intensifying crisis in our society also makes us aware of the need to analyse and understand it. We also refer literature more and more persistently to the social environment. Thus, we also become relevant to society and connect meaningfully with fellow human beings.

The "human" and "social" in literature become increasingly fused into a tangible artistic expression in which the mind of the artist with all its complexity, richness and mystery is revealed. We remember sitting in the class-room in the sixties listening to our teachers of English who explained first the "meaning" of lines, if it was a poem they taught, or the theme if it was a novel or a play. Teachers thought that the language would be a barrier for students and therefore dwelt upon the meanings, both lexical and contextual, of difficult words. Form was something teachers did not know what to do with. Conceptually, it was supposed to be a means through which meaning would be expressed. The three unities were brought in, in the case of drama teaching, but were called unnecessary since very few writers, including Shakespeare, stuck to them. In poems, similes and metaphors were taken apart and analysed and the interpretation was referred to the central message or idea that the poet wanted to communicate. There were occasionally comments on images and symbols but what was said was more or less the same as about similes and metaphors and related to the central idea in the same manner. In the drama and the novel, the beginning, the middle and the end, the plot and sub-plots, the characters with the kind of roles they played and "diction," all categories of nineteenth century criticism, were taken up separately and dealt with.

Two specific points — linked with each other at a deeper level, also emerged during teaching. The first related to the romantic notion that all one saw at work in texts was to reveal the mind and sensibility of the writer which imparted organic wholeness to the literary work. The second emphasized the psychological dimension, another manifestation, as is clear, of the same romantic viewpoint that the writer's mind worked in mysterious ways vis-a-vis the pressures, temperamental, familial, societal, that hung on him. The important thing was that all details in the text were supposed to offer clues to the beliefs and opinions the writers had evolved while interacting with their immediate environment. Thus the message and meaning that teachers brought out and explained during the sixties and earlier was connected with the biographical element — writers sought to convey a particular message because they imbibed certain aspects of life and culture from their background.

We can see quite clearly today that the first point brought out the relationship, though in an elementary way, between the writer and his work — how the work came to be conceived and given shape; while the second drew attention to the writer's relationship with his family and social background, his general environment. Quite obviously also, the first was a slight advance on the latter's perspective which had roots in the eighteenth century emphasis on a writer's life and personality. It gave a new dimension to the study of literature. According to it, there was a way in which the process of imbibing social reality, and imparting aesthetic structure to it could be understood and analysed. Samuel Johnson's critical essays, he aptly termed them "Lives," only offered

INTRODUCTION

a mechanistic idea of the creative process. Johnson believed that moral and educative aspects gave impetus to the writer's endeavour and that the writer was obliged in his own peculiar way and through the artistic form he chose to adopt to fulfil a socio-cultural obligation. It could never occur to a typical eighteenth century mind that the creative process was a complex psychological phenomenon, something that romantic writers highlighted later. It is a different story though that writers and thinkers of the eighteenth century were extremely relevant to their conditions as they were rooted in them.

This was the background to the perspective of English teaching in our Universities till the early sixties, a perspective that drew almost unconciously upon two different literary approaches and made them a part of the working arrangement called the teaching of literature.

Do we feel surprised that as late as the middle of the twentieth century in India, English literary writing was not understood in relation to the background against which it had emerged ? A whole lot of thinking along lines ranging from psychological-anthropological to Marxist on such a relationship had been done in the first four decades of our century. Is it then that our teachers had not kept themselves abreast of the critical developments in the country of our colonial masters ? If we look at the process closely, we find that English studies had for a long time been pursued in our country with the aim that the educated Indians become familiar with the English literary landmarks, look in wonder upon the artistic heights scaled by larger-than-life sensibilities belonging to the metropolis. It is a tragic case that great humanists such as Shakespeare, Milton and Wordsworth were sought to be used, and successfully, by our colonial masters to project an image of superhuman grandeur and creativity. The purpose was best served when Indian students learnt to interpret them after crossing the essential barrier of language and idiom, in terms of abstract messages and themes. They rightly inculcated the habit of attempting "critical appreciation" and elucidation of the works of Great literary masters of English literature!

The question of relevance of English literature, of the meaning of works of the great literary masters of England for us in India was not raised with any seriousness. In fact, there always remained a gulf between the general needs and requirements that conditions in India generated and the values and traditions that our teachers and scholars projected through English studies. English works appeared to us as treasures of crystallized human experience worth looking upto and emulating in our behaviour as sensitive individuals. The high standard to be met was to conform to the western ways of thought idealised for us by our masters to suit their intellectual requirements. No wonder that most of us still engaged in the study of western literatures, English and American, wait for new critical approaches to be evolved by analysts of cultural-literary trends in the universities abroad. And we still lap up those approaches uncritically, our perceptions and responses being similar to the ones given out by our western counterparts. This would be clear from analyses and comments made by our English studies scholars, even the journals and magazines we edit and publish from different academic centres. This makes us so untrue, so unauthentic in our own surroundings.

There is a danger in the criticism we have made here of the English studies. If we allow ourselves to be swayed by nationalisic bias, we run the risk of slurring over the contradictions present in our own society. After all, there is a lot around us in our surroundings that needs a close scrutiny before we decide to adopt it to evolve with its help an approach useful for us in our pursuit of sound literary and aesthetic norms. Even the commonplace perceptions we have called "western" are not actually so alien that we say they have no roots here. We have a section in our society whose cultural and political interests coincide with the interests of world imperialism today. This section raises time and again the cry of nationalism, of Indianness, of our rich past heritage. It presents all issues in terms of East versus West. Our difference with their approach, as should be clear from our analysis, is that we look at the question of perspective related to English studies from the angle of an erstwhile colonised community still working to a large extent with old reflexes and not sufficiently aware of the pitfalls inherent in the approach we have adopted. Secondly, in our own society, our "position" has to be that which *identifies* us with the victims of our contradiction-ridden system, human beings living in extreme conditions of misery and exploitation. These people require not just basic amenities but rational-humanist thought as well as a culture and literature superior to the ones offered either by the upper strata of western socicities or our own. We also believe that great masters of western literatures including English literature — Shakespeare, Milton, Goethe, Balzac, Tolstoy and Whitman, to name just a few — are a part of that profound cultural tradition which our own writers like Tagore, Sarat Chandra, Mahashweta Devi and Prem Chand have further evolved through their intense involvement with the fate of the exploited humanity of their times. This positive literary-cultural tradition faces an enormous challenge from thinkers and critics driven by imperialist urges, be they in the form of psychologism, modernism or anti-industrialism. Such theories idealise and mystify literary experience entirely beyond the pale of rational-historical discourse. They seem to have been evolved particularly to work against the growth and development of a culture and literature and a viewpoint that are deeply rooted in the sense of justice, equality and dignity.

Our link with the rich Indian history in the nineteenth century is quite significant. We saw in this period a clash between the Indian ways of life and thought and British Imperialism. The clash occurred not merely in the economic field but also in areas of politics and culture. The efforts of British imperialists in pursuit of overall dominance were so determined, varied and planned (the English were relatively very advanced and developed in industry, science and technology as well as in military strategy) that the struggle between the two powers was heavily weighted on the side of England. When we say "two powers," we simplify matters. India was not one homogeneous or unified politico-social entity in the nineteenth century, its centre of Mughal authority having weakened over a period of time. Nationalism struck roots in our country only towards the end of the nineteenth century. Even till the break of the First World War, we were not aware, except in a hazy manner, who our enemy was. It is a different matter that the nationalist struggle became so intense in the nineteen twenties that Indian masses learnt in political awareness in days and weeks what normally they would have learnt in months and years. But that came later. If we see a drastic change in the life conditions in India in the nineteenth century — a spate of famines which were man-made, devastation of indigenous production, and consequent impoverishment of the Indian masses — it is because we as a country and community found it impossible to withstand the challenge and pressure of British imperialism.

On the other side, conditions in the nineteenth century England were not exactly stable or happy. A large number of English population had concentrated in the urban centres. Villages and small towns did not offer to their inhabitants proper means of livelihood. We know of this from the novels of Dickens, and from that revealing book of F. Engels, *The Condition of the Working Class in England*. Hardy's novels, too, tellingly bring out the plight of the poor industrious folk in the countryside. *Tess* and *The Mayor of Casterbridge* are not just literary masterpieces conveying the sense of growing isolation and tragedy of their protagonists but also sociological documents informing readers about the exploitation of the English working masses in large agricultural farms — symbols of modernisation of productive processes! In fact, Charles Dickens's anguish and Hardy's tragic vision can be better grasped if we place their works against the conditions of existence in England in the nineteenth century.

This makes the picture for us quite complex and intricate. We as victims of British Imperialism in the nineteenth century have to comprehend the essence of dominance by an alien country determined to squeeze out our economic strength and social vitality. At the same time, we have to understand the aggressiveness of the British endeavours in the context of sharp antagonisms in their own society — they at that point of time are desperately in search of resources in the colony to overcome their own crisis. The pressures generated by this crisis turned the erstwhile idealistic and dynamic bourgeois class of England into a ruthless pursuer of economic gains and therefore insensitive towards the higher principles of honesty, fair dealing, equality and fellow-feeling. The nineteenth century writers on the other hand, great humanists as they are, feel one with the suffering people of their country and present negative images of the powers that be. This would bring the masses in the colony quite close to the underprivileged and suppressed people of the metropolis. Nineteenth century English writing, more than that of our own, has seeds of such a humanism. Hence our selection, in the beginning of the series, of the nineteenth century writing for analysis and comment.

Periodisation always throws up questions about what is to be included and what is to be excluded. With Said hovering in the background we are ever conscious of the ideology behind such constructions. We would like to clarify at the outset that we do not think that there is something monolithic about what is called the nineteenth century literature. Even as there are significant ruptures which serve as markers for a new age, yet historical changes are slow and the dialectics of change don't necessarily work out in a linear fashion. In using the phrase nineteenth century literature, we expect there to be many discontinuities and contradictions in the texts belonging to this period. Yet the use of this term is not entirely arbitrary or without relevance to us. Even as it restricts the chronological limits of the texts at one level, yet at another level it brings to the fore the positions from which we have examined the texts, not all of which remain within that limit.

For us it marks the entrenchment of the imperialist rule and subsequently the formation of modern India. The intro-

INTRODUCTION

duction of English studies in the curriculum, both in England and in India took place then. It also signals the beginning of the national movement and hence the inclusion of an interview with a historian, Bipan Chandra, in order to examine certain aspects of the national movement and their link to modern day politics. The attempt is to bring to the fore the forces that go towards creating the postions from which these articles emerge and put all the articles into the larger discourse of nationalism and colonialism in order to understand what the study of literature means to us today, even as we are conscious that any article on literature has to now also combat problems of historiograpy in order to define its own position. In fact that is the subject of one of the papers included here, Sanjay Kumar's "Fiction or Historical Positioning?: A Reading of J.G. Farrell's *The Siege of Krishnapur.*"

Farrell's novel, set against the events of 1857, raises interesting questions on what constitutes a novel based on historical facts and a document on history. Distinctions between narrativiser and narrator become problematic when they both deal with the same historical materials to frame their narrative. The paper also throws up problems regarding the hierarchical order of what constitutes evidence.

It is on the question of evidence that uncovering the history of the development of English studies in India creates problems. We remain bothered about finding "facts" and "evidence of the teaching process" so that we can interpret them. As a result it is easier to write about Macaulay's Minutes than it is to discuss how the "natives" received this education. Therefore, our historical studies often take recourse to personal recollections or what goes into forming the collective memory. P.K. Dutta's paper, "Keats' Odes: Learning and Teaching," is a peep into what went into classroom teaching, through the eyes of a student, who later went on to become a teacher, against the unfolding of various events which shaped the changing responses to Keats.

The dynamism that constitutes classroom teaching remains very often unrecorded and hence we have little evidence on how various teachers at various moments in history have tried to negotiate the gap between what they are expected to teach and what the students respond to. Zakia Pathak's paper, "Writing in Ourselves" foregrounds another important aspect of classroom teaching, where the teacher continually tries to mediate between the reality in the text and the social reality in which the teaching takes place, in order to bring "meaning" into teaching.

The desire to bring "meaning" into teaching is something that has haunted most teachers for nearly thirty years of their academic careers. It raises questions on what should be the contents of the syllabus. Is their something called a "significent text" or a "major writer," which or who has to always figure in the syllabus? Can Shakespeare be unrepresented in a course on English Literature? To understand this we have included three papers on such "great" writers — Charles Dickens and Henry James.

Sambudha Sen's "The Idea of Poverty in the Novels of Dickens" focuses on an issue that perturbs all of us in India in some way or the other. It brings to the fore the way a writer analyses and depicts poverty in his novels. It is perhaps another area of research to see whether the reading of such literature sensitizes us to our own reality or it is the readings which sensitize us to the issues in the text.

Kumkum Sangari takes up James' *Wings of the Dove* to show how polysemy can be skilfully used to position a reader to extract a predictable understanding of the text. By foregrounding the gaps and silences within the text she elucidates how narratives which apparently seem open to multiplicity can actually evade and even conceal areas which can jeopardise the smooth flow of the narrative.

O.P. Grewal focuses upon the problem of interpretation. He places F.R. Leavis' understanding of *Hard Times* in our own cultural context and goes into the relevance of a critical response in the light of ideological predilections that inform it. Grewal comments that Leavis' stand is not adequate to bring out the colonial perspective of exporting literary traditions based on the works of a great writer of the metropolis.

* *Mohua Lahiri*
* *Sanjay Kumar*
* *Anand Prakash*

2

Keats' *Odes:* Learning & Teaching

P.K. Dutta

I left Calcutta in 1972 when it was still simmering. The Marxist movement there, the biggest and most enthusiastic in the country since Telengana, was in shambles. The Naxalites and the CPI(M) were in a state of war. On the other hand, the State was slowly gaining strength through police repression and Congress (I) workers. To me, a non-political, anti-Marxist adolescent, the only meaning of mass movements and politics seemed to be violence. Nationally, popular discontent was being assimilated and reformulated into the populist consensus of "Garibi Hatao." Though I was non-political, I could not help but register the disenchantments of the time, their burden being felt all that more, possibly because like other adolescents in my circumstance, I had centred my life in rock music. Western popular music was still an utterly encompassing experience. It still held forth the promises of the 60's: Woodstock, a counter-culture, a vision. More than anything else, rock music was radically, and often undiscriminatingly, discontented with the terms of its existence. There was then for me, a metaphor with which to absorb the growing sullenness of popular life in Calcutta, while of course remaining distant from it.

I discovered Keats in Delhi, as an uprooted person. Contrary to established theories of despair and homelessness as created by the heterogeneity of urban life, the homeliness of Calcutta springs precisely from its intimate juxtapositions of widely - varied relationships, spaces and objects. On the other hand lay Delhi, just starting to blossom into the most conspicuously opulent and powerful city in the country. Big empty roads, pretty houses with rectangular lawns, a vision of vast symmetrical space marginalising its history into a "walled city," waiting to be filled with ambitions and hopes, without the problems of relating to a collective life. I lived a binary opposition. Calcutta, animated, collective life suffering from a disenchantment which was now reinforced by my nostalgia for all of it, and the order and elemental spirit of opportunity in Delhi.

I cannot remember how much of this predicament was displaced on to Keats and shaped by him. But I do remember that Keats became very important for me, my relationship with his poems, especially the *Odes*, an article of faith. This was made possible by the way I was taught Keats. I would like to dwell here on my teacher.

His interpretation of Keats seemed straightforwardly teleological. Looking back, however, I can sense that this teleology rested on a cyclical movement. His gurus were two books by J. Middleton Murry, the pages of which were grey with repeated perusal. He hated T.S.Eliot and F.R. Leavis, and looked at New Criticism with contempt. For him only Murry could express the indissoluble state of experience which Keats lived and wrote. It was an experience which my teacher lived every year, converting the vision of a poet professing towards illumination into a cyclical one with every fresh batch of students. The amazing thing was that, contrary to the stereotype of teaching, he did this without the least anxiety of boredom. Repetition for him, especially when teaching Keats, was not categorized as boring institutional practice. For him it was a necessary act of confirmation.

He used *Endymion* as a starting point. There were two aspects he dwelt on, which for him were really one. The first was Keats' adolescence, which he regarded paternally as a period of playfulness, of exuberantly testing poetic powers without any sense of commitment. The second related aspect was Keats' sensuousness, where he recalled Spenser's influence, elaborated on ideas of synaesthesia, and which he regarded positively as laying the basis of Keats' poetic sensibility. But *Endymion* was clearly not his interest. It was merely the background, a necessary introduction to the childhood of the poet.

The *Odes* for him marked a qualitative shift. What impressed him most was the desperate commitment to understanding that Keats developed as he battled through the antagonisms of his society, his lover and his critics, and came face to face with certain death. For my teacher the year 1819 was a wonderful time when the poet changed from adolescent to adult, from playfulness to high seriousness.

It was "Ode to a Nightingle" which he saw as the bridge between these two broad phases in Keats' life and poetry. The first two stanzas he regarded as a throwback to the early period of sensuousness and irresponsible pleasure through which Keats was attempting to escape from the burden of his growing understanding of life detailed in Stanza III. It was Stanza IV that he regarded as the turning point in Keats' life, when the latter decides that Art is the only serious way of coming to terms with his existence, seeing in Stanza V the clarity of vision which imagination gives the poet, and in Stanzas VI and VII the joyful and wise self-forgetfulness that is achieved through Art which according to my teacher, was the obverse, contrasting state of escape offered by the first two stanzas. Art was, for my teacher, by definition serious and therefore the real discriminating mark between fairly similar states of consciousness. Finally, he saw Keats' failure to forget himself in the nightingale as a partial one, the last two lines of Stanza VIII exemplifying the condition of "purgatory blind," the poetic state of suspense antecedent to the really great insights and achievements of Art.

The Stanza that my teacher explicated at length, besides the last one (which he used as an introduction to Keats' poetic theory of "Negative Capability") was Stanza III. What he expanded upon was the ache of impermanence accentuated by the more particular problem of social and sexual disregard that Keats experienced. It was this double burden of temporality that he regarded as the sub-text of "Ode on a Grecian Urn," his favourite poem. What attracted him most about this poem was that it appeared to offer an experience of Negative Capability in the sublimated experience of appreciating the Urn. It was a total, autonomous celebration of permanence which he found in the first three stanzas. The submerged situational context of the poem, of the poet going aroud the urn, he offered as only a detail of the glossary. Nor did he dwell too elaborately on the death-like quality of impermanence which Keats suggests in Stanza IV, confining himself to simply explicating it as the necessary qualification to the self-sufficiency of Art.

For my teacher,"Ode on a Grecian Urn" was central to Keats' poetry because it dealt with the key issues of permanence/impermanence, the necessity of artistic endeavour, and the inevitable social indifference that receives these efforts. But more than anything else, the "Ode on a Grecian Urn" contained what was for him the two most significant lines in Keats' poetry '"Beauty is truth, truth beauty'...need to know." He must have spent at least two classes on these lines.

The strange thing is I can recall only vaguely what he had to say. My overwhelming impression was that of a complicated argument. What I distinctly remember was his dismissal of the interpretation that Keats was establishing an equivalence between life and art. If I remember correctly his argument was that the ideal of Beauty was real insofar as that the aspiration towards permanence was a truth about the human condition, but that the reality of living life was equally beautiful. In this paradox I think he resolved, or at least put together two conflicting relationships with Keats. For my teacher the lines -

> When old age shall this generation waste,
> Thou shalt remain, in midst of other woe
> Than ours, a friend to man...

were of extreme significance for his own relationship with Keats as well as his relationship with his students. My teacher was an old man, verging on retirement, with only his students' developing minds to bear the imprint of his own all-embracing relationship with Keats. On the other hand, he could not overlook the qualification "Cold Pastoral," for he was firmly convinced that the Art-Life divorce limited the ability of art to "live": it produced an inferior art and inhibited a full knowledge of life. He was sure that it was this recognition which made Keats write his most important poem, "Ode to Autumn."

The "Ode on Melancholy" did not occupy too much of his attention. He saw in it a firm rejection of the urge towards youthful escapism and the prelude towards discovering permanence in the living world. For my teacher, the basis for "Ode to Autumn," was in that the poet was able to recognize the co-existence of joy and the sorrow, the delight of the moment along with a recognition of its passing.

He regarded "Ode to Autumn" as the pinnacle of Keats' understanding, in that Keats finally comes to accept life. The quality of acceptance was for him crucial. It bridged the gap between Life and Art. By accepting life, the poet was freed from the burden of idealising the permanence of Art as counter to the temporariness of existence. It permitted Keats to recognise the permanence vested in Art as co-extensive with the permanence of Life, a move that was enabled by Keats accepting the world of nature and man as a continuous process. Finally, in this quality of acceptance my teacher found Keats to equal Shakespeare's vision of life. He would compare it to what he regarded as the finest moment in the greatest work of art written by the greatest poet, that of Cordelia replying "No cause, no cause" to Lear's enquiry as to whether she had any complaints against him.

There was not very much in this interpretation that was original. On the contrary, in his emphasis on suffering and acceptance, he could very well be seen as repeating the pieties of English Literary Criticism. More than this, when he talked about suffering and acceptance, it was to denote qualities that could not be shared with mainstream society which was too busy "getting and spending." Such a vision could easily be seen as a reproduction of the long line of literary critics from Arnold (if not from the Romantics themselves) who argued for English Literary Criticism as a necessary and privileged enclave of people trained to feel and evaluate their world. There was in his relationship with us, his students, an attempt to create an aristocracy of sensibility.

He could, in short, be seen as a passive product of the colonial enterprise which sought to create natives in the image of their masters or worse, their masters' ideas about them. But such an understanding could at best be only partial. He was for one, in appearance — clad in dark khadi and chappals — very much the reverse of the public school-bureaucratic-executive image of smartness. His looks identified him as much more rooted in the specific high culture of Uttar Pradesh. His hospitality, when one visited him, revealed the same roots. He was highly conversant with Hindi literature, was acquainted with Sanskrit, probably understood Urdu even if he did not speak it: in short a person who was rooted in different cultures. The problem was that when he taught Keats, he hardly ever referred to his knowledge of other cultures. There was in him an inherited conservatism that insisted on a rigid separation between the cultures of different languages, a separation that arose from the need to accommodate the patriotisation of culture which insisted that no linguistic culture could be understood apart from the soil of its origin and nurture.

But such an assumption was bound to create problems, since his interpretation of Keats was so insistent on the connections between life and art. And in fact the continuing strand in his lectures was a constant antithesis between the preoccupations of the artists and the banality of the commercial world. And it was at these points that his generalisation on Keats would begin, and he would go on to dwell on the money grubbers of Delhi. This was no formal rhetoric for him. He was an exception in his family which traditionally dealt in commerce. It was as intimate and real as that.

The way I think he brought these two spaces and histories together, that of early nineteenth century England and of his own life in a Delhi College was in the mode of his delivery. This was probably the most striking thing about his lectures, what I remember most about them. He exuded intensity. Not only was his voice intense as it read out the poems, it remained so during the rest of his lecture. And this was backed by a glowing gaze that demanded complete absorption. It was this which made his understanding so convincing. For it was only the experience of rapture that could permit a certain simplicity of structure by which complex interwinings of histories and appropriations could be lived and communicated effectively, as a single reflex.

Clearly he derived this mode of communication from Middleton Murry's style and possibly also from an extension of the idea of Negative Capability interpreted as an intense way of experiencing other selves, different emotions. But, equally, it recalled other traditions. The very choice of this form of teaching constituted an authority of its own that could receive modifications and suggestions but not possibly endure outright contradiction. There was thus authoritarianism in that voice. It was aligned to actions of dignity and distance. But it was not the authoritarianism of bureaucratic distance; it drew its energies from the more delicate operations of patriarchalism by which he created distance not through classifications but by an appeal to experience, and the specific knowledge of its inspired quality. He was a man who could give advice on more mundane matters outside the classroom. In short, he drew also on the idea of the Guru.

His embodiment of the Guru idea was not structured on discipline or simple obedience. In some ways the institutional structure of the education system did not quite allow that. But more than this, his tone could not be disciplinarian precisely because he was engaged in forging a common opposition with his student against the rampant commercialism of Delhi. His authoritarianism was also based on a profound discontent. The way he could resolve these relationships, was through eliciting emotional surrender from his students rather than obedience. In this he recalled yet another tradition, that of the National Movement. Whether it was Gandhi or the terrorists, the same problem confronted them both: how to combine the necessity of establishing a central authority while unleashing a general awakening. Their ways of course were very different. Gandhi demanded surrender to his conscience and inspiration, while the terrorists took recourse to the easier method of creating totalising symbols of Mother figures.

This idea of intense surrender to artistic experience was not something new to me as I had already been initiated into it through rock music. Nor was the idea of society as representing an outside zone of banal commerce intellectually stimulating. What was a discovery for me was that this intensity could be harnessed to objects and aims outside the self, and that there could be a movement within the terms of this general experience towards an affirmation of life. It did not necessarily make me more knowledgeable about my society, but it certainly made me more aware. It gave me a mooring in this new city, not only in my relationship with Keats and my teacher, but also with the few students who participated in this act of re-experiencing Keats' development.

The Emergency was a turning point in all our lives. For me it made the image of Calcutta when I left it inescapable. But unlike the Calcutta of the early 70s, the sullen anger generated by the growing list of depredation did not leave the upper classes nor any spaces in the country untouched. For the first time after the National Movement, there was a general recovery of purpose and political commitment which crystallized clearly after the Emergency was lifted. For me, Keats figured in all this. The idea of an intense commitment to Life outside oneself could lead easily to an identification of Life with society or at least those sections of society one regarded as the victims of ruling ethics, especially under the conditions of political Authoritarianism which made one realize, through its suppression, the possibilities of Life that society had and which was concealed by a simple-minded repudiation of it. I attended my first political meeting ever, when the Janata Party gave a general call to assemble at the Ram Lila Grounds. My relationship with a collective political life in Delhi began.

The paradox was that it was at this time that I found myself going away from Keats. Apart from the general image of him as a namby-pamby adolescent (which influenced me considerably), I was becoming more involved with the criticism of T.S.Eliot and F.R.Leavis and later with Brecht. This series of new involvements made me react severely to the fetishisation of intensity not only as inhibiting a critical attitude, but more importantly, as an inadequate response to the multi-faceted problems of relationships which any commitment to collective life demands.

Meanwhile there was the faliure of the Janata Government, the restoration of Indira Gandhi, the Delhi riots and finally the triumph of Rajiv Gandhi, who for a time became the lyrical, futuristic symbol of a middle class that had been surreptitiously proliferating in the last decade. On the other hand grew, as a consequence of the special applications of Thatcherism to our country, an ever-intensifying unrest in all spheres, involving us in Delhi University in three big strikes. All this while of course we shuddered under the shadows of international Right Reaction which under Reagan's leadership promised an utopia of utter annihilation.

Intellectually the mid-80s was an unstable but stimulating period. With the introduction of structuralism and more importantly semiotics, discourse analysis, together with the critiques of Feminism and Foucault, we in India received and set out to appropriate a radical extension in the field of political and cultural knowledge. This dovetailed with the impact of the riots and strikes in Delhi, which made the intelligentsia more generally preoccupied with collective action. On the other hand, these new ideologies/methodologies, especially of Foucault, opened up extremely perceptive critiques of Enlightenment, Rationality and accompanying institutional structures while depriving the idea of institutions—which was identified as the structure of society itself—any possibilities of allowing access to the idea of freedom.

It was with some surprise that I started teaching Keats in 1987. Surprise, because contrary to my expectation that all these developments would make of Keats a somewhat pitiful figure, I was confirmed in my adolescent experience of him as a powerful poet. What gave Keats a new significance was precisely these intervening developments. I rediscovered the fact that the Romantics were in fact the first to consciously interrogate the subject-object divide, the problems of which had first come to me through Subaltern Studies in their critiques of Positivism and more generally of Rationalism. I suddenly realized that none of us, not even the "great" Foucault himself had cared to register the self-evident other history of resistance to Rationalism. What was more striking was that Keats, as with the other Romantics was not merely preoccupied with resistance, but extended that into a search for an alternate epistemology. It seemed to me, that Keats was attempting to arrive at a new relationship between subject and object, without simply inverting the preoccupation from object to subject which the Subalterns tended to do, and on this basis create a vision of Life as possibility. This Keatsian notion of possibility at that point became very important to me not only on account of my ambiguous relationship with Foucault's critique but more fundamentally, because of terror inflicted by the Riots and the threat of nuclear annihilation.

I started my lectures with the usual background introduction on eighteenth century thought and politics, with a minor introduction to the pre-Romantics and expressed the fairly conventional and possibly simplistic idea of the pre-Ode phase as one of sensuousness. I classified the four odes into two groups, putting "Ode to a Nightingale" and "Ode on a Grecian Urn" into one block, the rationale being that in these two poems Keats attempts to achieve a relationship with the terms of his existence through mediations. What I explicated at greater length was the Keatsian notion of dialectics, inherent in its theory of Negative Capability. What struck me was that while Negative Capability was an original way of relating to the world, in terms of experiencing different and contradictory states of consciousness, its implicit passivity was replaced in the *Odes* by an active, conscious weighing of alternatives which were intensely and comprehensively experienced before being qualified or rejected.

The first three stanzas of "Ode to a Nightingale" I saw as the conscious setting up of the objective of self-forgetfulness, rather than a complete identification with the bird. What was interesting was that through the sensuous evocation of the Bacchanalian world, Keats was creating a larger context for this species of self-forgetting, by recalling the image of communitarian festivity. The third stanza was important because it qualified this path by reverting back to the world of temporality, disregard and anguish, a counter-movement that resulted implicitly from the unreachability of that festive community. What was important was that besides the sorrow, these lines emphasized the dullnes, the complete lack of possibility in such an existence. The fourth stanza was a reiteration of the consciousness of intentions, rather than a dissolution into aesthetic experience. "Poesy" here referred not simply to a general notion of Poetry (or how else are we to classify the preceding three stanzas ?), but indicated a different notion of Art that was grounded in a paradox. It let Keats to a consciousness of the world and the recreation of its possibilites; but this was achieved only in terms of seeing life as composed of natural processes devoid of human presence. The vulnerability of such a vision was underlined by the qualification "viewless," which suggested the critical paradox of the world of Stanzas IV and V, its idea of acceptance premised on shutting off the real, living world.

In the reconstitution of the dark night of the soul (Stanzas III & IV) the significance of the Nightingale as mediator between the poet and Life itself changed. From being the unreachable symbol of happiness, it became something in the nature of a sign necessary for the Self to renew its perception of possibility that extends not only to Life but also its negation, i.e. death. In Stanzas VII & VIII the paradox became a contradiction. The disappearance of the bird drew attention to its own tangibility and underlined the vulnerabilities of this ecstasy. Without, however, losing sight of the alterations wrought by the whole experience. The last two lines were not an aesthetic resolution of this contradiction, but a confirmation of the profounder connection between Life and Art which this experience had given him. It was in the form of question - "Was it a vision or a waking dream? Fled is that music, Do I wake or sleep?" - that expressed this particular experience of insubstantiality and clarity, implicitly underlining the problematic nature of the connection between Life and Art and thus opening up new demands on this relationship itself.

This view of existence as alternate possibilities in which the gap between the poet and the world outside him, between subject and object were bridged in different ways in order to confront problems of temporality and art, was given a new direction in "Ode on a Grecian Urn." It started with a resolution, developed a single possibility without however cancelling the force of opposition and contradiction. The urn as it was presented was shown to combine Life and Art, the illustrations and visuals on the urn together with the poet's palpable response to them. And in doing so, the experience of the urn combined many levels of antitheses within itself—passion and contemplation, joy and sorrow, temporality and permanence. In this there was a development from "Ode to a Nightingale," where contraries (e.g. temporality as possibility/end of possibility), were experienced as separate modes of perception. In the "Grecian Urn" Keats developed a poetic equipoise that combined them. What was interesting was that the inherent contradictions which were submerged by a vision of combination and unification, were allowed to implode the vision from within. This was prefigured in the situational context of the poem itself, which silently indicated the action of the poet going round the urn, suggesting in this still narrative of visuals the different movement of a living and animating being. What I liked about this definition of the urn as lifeless (Stanza IV) and lacking therefore in any source of life other than what the living can give to it, was Keats' absolute refusal, in fact, inability to treat an undoubtedly successfully epistemological achievement as an end in itself. At the same time there was no simple rejection of that experience—it was felt, understood and finally defined-"cold Pastoral"- which yet had the possibilities of warmth in the living friendship and thoughts a person could give to it. It was in this spirit that I interpreted the two lines--not as philosophy, or self-evident summary, but as ironic in the sense that it expressed the double-voicedness of this experience without offering a conclusion.

I did not spend too much time on "Ode on Melancholy" assessing its value for my lectures really as a curtain-raiser for "Ode to Autumn". It marked a shift from the other two *Odes* in that there was the absence of any mediations, indicating an urge to enter into a direct relationship with Life itself. However, the quality of the recognition of life as composed of contraries seemed somewhat aestheticized, the catalogue of sensory states replacing the comprehensive critical grappling with experience.

Like my teacher and countless other critics, I taught "Ode to Autumn" as the climax of Keats' poetic career. In it he identified life as process, which allowed him to reconcile the problems of life and death, time and timelessness. Moreover life was seen not as contingent on the poet's relationship with it, but something that includes humanity within it. In achieving this vision Keats was not only able to overcome the subject-object divide, but stood on the brink of reconceptualising the whole notion of the subject from the individual to a collective understanding of humanity. It was not a coincidence that natural processes were identified with peasants working on the land, not with Keats' relationship with Nature. What was most striking however was that the nature-man relationship was posited on the analogous conditions of natural activity and human labour. It was this notion of activity/labour that provided really the axis of the whole idea of process. It was in this context that one could see the original use of personification (if one could call it that) which Keats made. Personifications had earlier been used in English literature (Spenser, Pope, even in "Ode to Melancholy") to animate abstract values or conditions. In "Autumn," it was deployed to create and embody the basis of the relationship between Nature and Man through activity/labour. In the process nature was humanized, while man was naturalised. Death in this view became not the fact of mortality that created either anguish or desire, but the slow cessation of temporal activity that presented the promise of renewal as mystery and suggestiveness.

Sitting at the desk, I think I drew a great deal on the intense way which I had learned to cherish years ago in which my teacher had taught. There were also formulations I had borrowed from him : for one, the autobiographical structure itself. But there were new registers, different emphases, the notion of a critical epistemology drawing on dialectical thought, the emphasis on conflict, of the collective subject and labour and on celebration rather than an acceptance of life exemplified in "Autumn." Above all, there were new questions. Was the idea of Life as sheer possibility sufficient by itself or was the fact that Keats' autumn was detached from the imperatives of industry and political economy an aesthetic problem? Given the supposition that the idea of nature represented organicity was part of the international common sense of industrialising societies, was it not easier to find in the relationship with Nature a more harmonious and restful vision of existence? Or was the importance given to Nature prophetic, given the facts of Bhopal, Chernobyl and nuclear stockpiles? And finally, was the celebration of existence sufficient without the conception of struggle ?

What was Keats' relationship to Blake in whose poetry we find a marriage of the two?

Like my teacher I, too, tried to convert my class into an oppositional collective. But I attempted to break up the authoritarianism latent in the style of intense rendering I had inherited from my teacher, by banal witticisms and posing questions to students. Years later, I understood from an old student that I had not been successful. Being deluged with an intensive reading of Keats, they had merely written down eveything I had said, parrying my questions lightly with ill-considered replies. The breaks I had sought to introduce in my lectures had been merely regarded as the signature of my privilege: my achievement, it seemed to me, was to have bounded the desired role of a comrade by the image of the guru. Ultimately, despite my stress on the problems of a subject-object divide, I had, in my actual relationship with the students made them the passive subjects of my superior knowledge. Another problem dogged the inheritance from my teacher. I had failed to make my students conscious of how English Romanticism had imprinted itself within the literature and other discourses in our country. Neither a knowledge of regional literature nor possibly the inclination was available to me then. Most of all, I knew no history of ourselves by which I could place both my students and myself in our relationship with Keats.

Postscript

The point of this minor tale of my experiences of learning and teaching Keats' *Odes*, is to suggest that English literature Studies in our country, if I can presume to be some kind of a representative case, has had its own history. [It has fused with and reacted to critical schools in the West, but equally interacted with the problems and processes in our own country. Being altered in our reading of literature by these it in turn, offers opportunities for creating structures for understanding the fairly complex roads our country takes.] I mention this point, self-evident as it may be, to gesture at a lack of our knowledge of the history of English literature Studies in our country. It is to raise the problem of constructing this history. And in our particular branch of learning in this country—which has produced little by way of serious critical books, leave alone public debates—oral testimony would be an important source for such an enterprise. It would mark at least the beginning of understanding the conditions of transmission and appropriation of critical ideas originating in the west.

My recourse to History here is not to appeal to an extra-literary authority, but as a way of understanding the specific dynamics and particular characteristic of English literature Studies in our country. Clearly, English literature has outlived English rule and proliferated in independent India not only quantitatively but also by way of producing first class novels and poetry as well as a growing number of excellent theses. This fact must make us look again at the problem of how to relate political and economic power with cultural formation.

The problem of this relationship has recently surfaced again in a paradoxical phenomenon. Following the formulations of Said, a whole crop of critiques of colonial education have sprung up from mainly western universities, enabled to a large extent by financial structures controlled by the inheritors of our old colonial masters. Within the corpus of these highly competent scholars, possibly the most interesting and important work has been done by Gauri Vishwanathan in her book, *Masks of Conquest*. Her understanding of colonial educational policies in English literature Studies as evolving out of inner schisms, that are the product of nagging uncertainties about how to achieve colonial hegemony, is valuable. Less satisfying is her uncertainty about the way Indians responded to English literature. She concedes that this other history may be "immensely rich and complex," but that it remains apart from the colonial project. She gives her reasons in a somewhat perplexing formulation, saying that "if the colonial subject is a construct emanating from the colonizers' head,and therefore removed from history, the history to which the British administrator responds...is real only to the extent that it provides the rationale for his actions."[1] What may have been indicated above is the following: that there are two separate histories, that of the colonized and of the colonizer, and that the latter responded to the first only insofar as it confirmed their own discourse. That is to say, colonial hegemony was achieved by the sheer hermeneutic power of its own preoccupations. But this raises a problem: if the colonizer is only concerned with patting his own representation on the back, then clearly the consent that his hegemony seeks to elicit, would be one of willing surrender to his impositions. It may be noted here that Vishwanathan invokes the Gramscian idea of hegemony, as involving both force and consent, emphasizing in her work the second proposition. However if consent is a mode of surrender, then it follows that despite her acknowledgement of the Indian response as the narrative of a different initiative, she has in fact cancelled the implications of this assertion, by elliding the two separate components of Gramsci's definition.[2]

Such a reading of the relationship between English literature Studies and colonial hegemony, seems to me part of a longer common sense that has expressed itself in the self-description of pursuing English literature as submitting to an alien discipline. This self-image has traditionally been expressed in two ways. One is the path of self-flagellation, something that can only arise from a perceived recognition of guilt in willingly submitting to a "foreign" and therefore pathetic enterprise. Sisir Kumar Ghosh in a statement of utter self-repudiation describes the condition of English literature Studies thus: "A few lucky ones no doubt manage to escape, some even teach and publish abroad, the deferred dream of every brown boy at home. But generally speaking, we have reconciled ourselves to the role of the useless but self-important self-exile: else suppliers of footnotes to imported but ill-digested opinion that passes for wisdom."[3] Sisir Ghosh's response, it must be underlined, represents this self-image in a sensitive and introspective vein. The more usual response is to identify English literature as affording access to the social power that seems to have been encoded in the English language since British rule. Meenakshi Mukherji perceptively describes the character of the English language sub-culture in our campuses as the mark of "the new Brahmins of our campus elite, [who] stride confidently ahead to take charge of things."[4] Mukherji's observation goes one step further than Ghosh. What she gestures at is the way the English sub-culture has been internalised by the Indian elite, precisely because it spells both power and differentiation: that is, English (as both Language and Literature) has become Indian by virtue of its foreignness.

The basic assumptions of the self-image of English litterateur and his\her sub-culture, that underlies what both Ghosh and Mukherji have to say, is no doubt empirically verifiable and socially dominant. Of greater importance is the fact that both Ghosh and Mukherji seek to break this self-image, the first by advocating a study of comparative literature, the other by linking English teaching more forcefully with regional cultures. Both suggestions are important and their implementation, it may be added, is long overdue. Nevertheless the problem of their sufficiency still remains. For what they can ensure optimally is that the vocabulary of the elite self-image will change: it is less certain whether the basic paradigms and principles of construction of this self-definition will be altered.*

* Already a particular model of hybridisation is available in popular magazines such as *Stardust*, that combines English with Hindi (including Punjabi and Urdu words). Such cultural polysemicity remains as congealed as the "purer" English sub-culture in its mannered and stilted orientation, by which it proclaims the elitist character of its audience.

The point is that the hybridisation of English literature in our country is necessary, but we need to have a critical and creative notion of it. Here the little story of my teacher may be of some use, not by merely dramatising an interesting individual effort, but as revealing the trace of another history; one in which members of the English sub-culture have, in both clear and unresolved ways, attempted to position themselves in English literature, not only for sheer pleasure but also for its ability to provide a critical tool for interrogating other inherited cultures and situations. To understand this history a less limiting notion of hegemony needs to be acquired, in which consent is identified not merely with either willing submission or narrow utilitarian imperatives, but as also flowing from a willed appropriation of English literature to create the different ability of being able to relate critically to different hegemonic cultures,[5] a facility that may enable an open-ended view of culture itself, and involve a sturdy refusal to fetishize any culture in capital letters.

An oppositional history such as this may not have been constructed, but it is available. My teacher, for instance, could be seen as part of a longer lineage that includes a person like Derozio, for whom Romanticism was appropriated in acts of social sensation that scandalised conservative Hindu society, produced sometimes awkward, sometimes striking but always passionate poetry which revealed an early nationalism or celebrated the tragedy of Romeo and Juliet even as it ventured into love poetry that imitated Hafiz. Above all, what needs remembrance is the sheer joy of the sudden access to a different knowledge, that comes out even through the ordinariness of the following lines:

> Expanding like the petals of young flowers
> I watch the gentle opening of your minds,
> And the sweet loosening of the spell that binds
> Your intellectual energies and powers.
> (Sonnet to the Pupils of Hindu College)[6]

No doubt, as in all histories, there would be much that would strike an observer as misplaced, insufficient or even reactionary. But, then, any historical reconstruction needs to confront its own embarrassments in order to remind itself of the fallibility of its own preoccupations. More imperative is the need to see this history as process of critical cultural experimentations. Thus, for instance, such a history could equally confront the efforts of Michael Madhusudan Dutta, whose *Meghnadbadh* represented both a break from his preoccupation with the English language, while drawing on what he perceived as Milton's idealisation of Satan to turn the tables of morality against Ram in his own epic. But then a study of Madhusudan Dutta would involve yet another related enquiry into the problem of translations. The point that I am making here is a simple one, that this alternate history demands the serious, and hopefully constant, consideration of new possibilities of academic enterprise. And in this, I think, lies the final paradoxical triumph of my teacher : that his teaching raises the possibilities of a learning which he himself did not know.

Notes

1. Both citations are from Gauri Vishwanathan, *Masks of Conquest: Literary Study and British Rule In India* (London: Faber and Faber, 1989), p. 12.
2. When Vishwanathan does mention the Indian response (in its positive capacity), she sees it purely in terms of the response of the Indian elite in its role as elite, that is one which identifies English Literature in an Utilitarian way, as offering an avenue of power. This suggests that the Indian response operates within the parameters laid down by the colonial authorities, even while it may not internalise everything the English sought to impart. See. p. 44, *ibid.*
3. Sisir Kumar Ghosh,"The Future of English Studies in India: A Note,"in*English and India: Essays Presented to Proressor Samuel Mathai on his seventieth birthday*, ed. M.Manuel, K.Ayyappa Paniker (Madras:The Macmillan Co. Of India Ltd., 1978) p. 153.
4. Meenakshi Mukherjee, "Teaching Literature to a Sub-Culture,"*ibid*, p. 126.
5. At one point, Vishwanathan does mention the critical appropriation of colonial education when she remarks upon how its critique of Hinduism was generalised by some students of Hindu College into a critique of all Religion including Christianity. While this does enlarge the scope of Vishwanathan's thesis at an observational level, it may be remarked that the activity of these students went beyond criticising religion alone. Further, Vishwanathan identifies this as a solitary happening, isolable because the Indian response, which was overdetermined by colonialism, changed once the policies were altered. See p.77, *op. cit.*
6. All references to Derozio's work are from *Poem of Henry Louis Vivian Derozio: A Forgotten Anglo-Indian Poet* (Calcutta: Oxford University Press, 1923 rpt.1980).

3

The Idea of Poverty in the Novels of Dickens

Sambudha Sen

Dickens' career as a writer spans the forty odd years during which industrial capitalism first confronted the problem of mass urban poverty and then succeeded in marginalising it. When Dickens began writing, mass poverty was very much a part of "the condition of England," so intense and widespread that it was easily capable of pushing the British nation into the "chaos" of revolution. By the early fifties, however, the industrial economy had consolidated itself. This not only brought about a significant reduction in the intensity and scale of poverty, it also provided the mid-Victorian establishment with the justification for classifying those who failed to climb out of the world of workhouses and slums as "the residuum," "the sunken sixth,"--a race apart, morally and even biologically incapable of participating in the processes of "progress." In this essay I hope to chart Dickens' changing response to poverty, from the way he grapples with the very real,"here and now" problem of the poor in the early works, to the deeply subversive images, symbols, principles of plot construction that the (by now marginalised) world of poverty continues to generate in the later novels. Such an exercise is I hope not without interest, since poverty is a real issue in our part of the world even if it is something of a non-issue in Dickens'.

> Wretched, defrauded, oppressed, crushed human nature lie in bleeding fragments over the face of society...Every day that I live I thank heaven that I am not a poor man with a family in England.[1]

This is the American Colman describing his impressions of Manchester in 1845. Most modern historians would agree that Colman's words express the spontaneous horror that the condition of the urban poor evoked in contemporary observers. In its initial stages the industrialization of England meant extreme hardship for a very large number of her people. The precariousness of the industrial economy-based as it was on the production of a single item, textile[2]--itself implied both low wages and uncertain employment for the worker. Moreover industrialization deprived many artisans and petty tradesmen of their traditional modes of livelihood. What aggravated the material impoverishment of the worker (both industrial and non-industrial) was his/her social and human degradation. Herded in a hideous urban slum, very often without the means of subsistence, the dispossessed worker often found himself/ herself, as Engels put it, "losing more and more of [his/her] power to resist the demoralising influence of want, filth and evil surroundings."[3]

Although the English ruling classes were not exactly distinguished by their concern or sympathy for the poor, poverty in the first half of the nineteenth century was just too intense and widespread to be ignored. A measure of the fears and guilt that the poor aroused in the middle class was the treatment of poverty in the contemporary novel. Novelists of the early nineteenth century turned to the problem of poverty with a frequency and seriousness probably unsurpassed in the history of English literature.[4] "All the age," insisted Charles Kingsley in *Alton Locke,* "is tending in the direction of democratic art; in Landseer and his dogs -- in Fielding and his downs, with a host of fellow artists -- and in all authors who have seized the nation's mind, from Crabbe and Burns and Wordsworth to Dickens and Hood, the great tide sets ever towards, outwards towards that which is common to the many, not that which is exclusive to the few." An important, even decisive aspect of "that which is common to the many," was the experience of poverty, and it is to poverty that Alton must turn if he has to create "poetry of reality." As Sandy Mackaye, the radical bookseller puts it:

> That puir lassie dying on her bare board and seeing her savior in her dreams, is there na poetry in that callant? The sister prostituting herself to buy food for her freen--is there na poetry there?

Dickens would certainly have understood Sandy Mackaye. In a letter to Mrs. Gore, Dickens comes out militantly against those who might object to the realistic treatment of poverty in the novel, against the likes of Lord Melbourne who objected to *Oliver Twist* on the grounds that "It was all among Workhouses, and Coffinmakers, and Pickpockets"[6]:

> I have seen in different towns in England, and to see in London whenever I walk in its byways at night, as I often do, such miseries and horrors among the poor... that these aristocratic dolls do make me sick.

You see which side *I* am on. I can't help it. It's more genteel to be on the other side, but Truth doesn't always keep its carriage, and is sometimes content to go in hobnailed shoes and wheel barrows.[7]*

While it is important not to take statements like "you see what side I am on" at face value, poverty does in fact, emerge as an insistent theme in Dickens' early novels. There are two, and as it seems to me, contradictory levels at which Dickens delineates the poor in the early works. At the first level Dickens' whole strategy seems to be to use every possible novelistic means to provide compensations for the "horrors and miseries" that the poor suffer in real life. Thus it is precisely in the homes of the "deserving poor" that the famous Dickensian conviviality finds most frequent expression, enveloping the world of the Pegottys, the Trotty Vecks, the Cratchits in what Chesterton called the "Christmas spirit;" in that warm, informal feeling of relatedness and brotherly love of which the most stable site is the family. The family is, in fact, the second "humanising" agent in the early Dickens' representation of the poor. Dissociated from the responsibilities as much as from the class antagonisms of the larger public world, the family encourages the practice of the domestic virtues, the maintenance within the home of cleanliness and household order; and in this sense provides an idealised private space within which the "deserving poor" can be integrated to the "good" middle class world.

In his early novels Dickens uses various techniques to relieve, even glamorize the reality of poverty. He uses motifs from fairy tales and adventure stories as in the delineation of the Pegotty boathouse, genial humour that creates an atmosphere of warm informality in the otherwise drab homes of the poor. and, above all, the festive occasion to colour and contain within its spirit of joyous bonhomie the difficulties that the poor face in the real world. At least two early novels which deal directly with the poor are structured around the festive occasion. In *The Chimes* and *A Christmas Carol* Christmas and New Year's day become the means of resolving the protagonists' worldly difficulties, of creating a situation which can both keep off the troubles of the world outside and at the same time constitute itself as the core around which a happy

---

* Unlike Mrs. Gaskell or Benjamin Disraeli, Dickens does not deal with the industrial working class at least not until *Hard Times*. Yet as in *Mary Barton* or *Sybil* the problem of poverty is not only shown to be central to the condition of England question but is also linked causally to the policies and ideologies of the industrial bourgeois. In this sense while Dickens' early novels do not deal directly with industrial workers, it is impossible to delink the urgency with which the early Dickens treats the poor from the first and harshest phase of the Industrial Revolution.

benevolent community can take shape. When Trotty wakes up, after having dreamt of a nightmarish but eminently possible situation overtake his daughter, he not only finds Meg sewing her wedding gown but also that it is New Year.

> Before Will Fern could make the least reply, a band of music burst into the room, attended by a lot of neighbours, screaming 'A Happy New Year Meg!' 'A Happy Wedding!' 'Many of 'em!'...
>
> 'Trotty Veck, my boy! It's got about, that your daughter is going to be married tomorrow. There an't a soul that knows you and don't wish her well. Or that knows you both, and don't wish you both all the happiness the new year can bring.
>
> (TC,pp.160-61)*

The "deserving poor" sustain their domestic idyll not simply by their high spirits but also, more substantially, by the practice of hard work, prudence, orderliness, cleanliness, in short, by the practice of the classic middle class virtues. This brings us to an interesting disjunction in Dickens' delineation of the "deserving poor." Middle class values are so integral to the behaviour of Dickens' "deserving poor" that Louis Cazamian argued, not unreasonably, that the Pegottys, Cratchits, Nubbles belong to the lower middle class.[8] But, as one of the finest historians of the nineteenth century poor has shown, if income is the criterion, Dickens' poor folk can "by no stretch of the imagination... be regarded as lower middle class." For example, the Cratchit family, with eight mouths to feed on little more than a pound a week, would be worse off than "most working class families of the time," while the combined monthly wages of Kit and his mother would be below that of "the lower ranks of the working clsses." In terms of their earnings, and in terms of regularity of available work, the bulk of Dickens' poor belong to the casual non-industrial work force, that is, precisely to that section which would be exposed to the most brutalising effects of poverty. If Dickens' poor protagonists are protected from these effects it is because they have middle class traits grafted on to their personalities. The temptation of such grafting is easy to understand in an age when middle class modes of behaviour had begun to assume enormous moral importance in the popular consciousness. As Gertrude Himmelfarb puts it:

> It is perhaps no accident that at the very time the condition of working class women and children was seen as most grievous, middle class women were

---

* Charles Dickens, *A Christmas Carol and The Chimes* (London: Dent and Sons Ltd. 1980), pp. 160-61. All subsequent references are to this edition of the novel, and page numbers are given in the text parenthetically following quoted passages.

being exalted as paragons of virtue and domesticity, and middle class children as models of decorum and obedience. With factories, mines, and slums conjuring up visions of a Hobbesian state of nature, with political economy appearing to legitimise the laws of the jungle and Malthusianism holding out the prospect of unending misery and vice, it became more than ever necessary to assert the values of decency, propriety, and chastity " to remoralise what had been so fearfully demoralised.[10]

To make the poor respectable, to draw them into a moral economy of "decency, propriety and chastity" is at the heart of Dickens' delineation of the "deserving poor," and it is evident in the portrayal of Kit Nubbles and his mother, for example:

> The room in which Kit sat himself down in this condition was an extremely poor and homely place, but with an air of comfort about it, nevertheless, which " the spot must be a wretched one indeed " cleanliness and order can always impart in some degree. Late as the Dutch clock showed it to be, Kit's mother was still hard at work at the ironing table; a young child lay sleeping in a cradle near the fire; and another, a sturdy boy of two or three years old, with a very tight nightcap on his head and a nightgown much too small for him on his body.*

Interestingly "the cleanliness and order" overlays "the extremely poor condition of the room" with an air of comfort, and the genially comic mode transforms what ought to have been signifiers of poverty — "the very tight nightcap," for instance — to something that suggests cheery forbearance as well.

What makes Dickens' early novels more than a middleclass attempt to contain the problem of poverty, is that characters like Trotty Veck and the Nubbles occupy only a part, indeed a small part of the world of Dickens' poor. The "Christmas spirit" or the practice of the middle-class domestic virtues might protect Mrs. Nubbles or Bob Cratchit from the most brutalising implications of their poverty; the constitution of a special category of "the deserving poor" might even be said to make everybody else undeserving of sympathy; but clearly all this does not exhaust the problem of poverty in Dickens' early novels. It is not merely that "the deserving poor" are always exposed to the danger of sinking into "misery and Vice," as Trotty Veck's nightmare so powerfully dramatizes, or that Stephen Blackpool finds his stable life disrupted by the reappearance of an alcoholic wife. What is more, the demoralised, dispossessed poor are an insistent, overwhelming presence in Dickens' early novels. Indeed if we leave aside the great comic

---

* Charles Dickens, *The Old Curiosity Shop* (London: Penguin, 1972), p. 131. All subsequent references are to this edition of the novel and page numbers are given in the text parenthetically following quoted passages.

characters, the early Dickens' most unforgettable writing involves the outcasts of society - the imprisoned debtors in *The Pickwick Papers,* the inmates of the parish workhouse in *Oliver Twist,* the unwanted children incarcerated in Dothboys Hall in *Nicholas Nickleby.* Nor are the scenes of suffering confined within the four walls of a prison or a workhouse. The London of Dickens' early novels overflows with descriptions of the most grinding kind of poverty. *Sketches by Boz* is full of descriptions of London slums, with their wretched houses, overflowing drains, pawnbrokers and gin shops. The placid atmosphere of the *The Pickwick Papers* is punctuated with Sam Weller's account of "the worn out, starving, houseless creatures as rolls themselves in the dark corners o'lonesome places."* The first eleven chapters of *Oliver Twist* take the reader through a world of the most appalling kind of poverty and ugliness, a world where life is cheap and suffering general.

The demoralised poor are, however, more than a ubiquitous presence. They directly inspire some of Dickens' best early writing. "The Stroller's Tale" in *The Pickwick Papers* is a good example of Dickens' ability to enter into the tortured consciousness of the degraded poor. A habitual drunkard, the stroller has throughout beaten his wife and starved his children. But on his death bed Dickens shows him suddenly terrified of his docile and long suffering wife:

> 'There's something in her eyes that wakes such a dreadful fear in my heart, that it drives me mad. All last night, her large staring eyes and pale face were close to mine; whenever I turned they turned, whenever I started up from sleep, she was at the bedside looking at me. Jem she must be an evil spirit - a devil. Hush! I know she is. If she was a woman she would have died long ago. No woman could have bourne what she has... I beat her Jem, I beat her yesterday and many days and many times before. I have starved her and the boy too; and now that I am weak and helpless she'll murder me for it.
>
> (*PP.* 140)

There is no attempt here to protect the reader from the horror of the situation. On the contrary, the stroller's critical situation becomes the means of raising to a nightmarish level of intensity the want, the alcoholism, the violence which, as all Commissions of Inquiry Reports agreed, were pervasive in the slums. But what makes this scene particularly unbearable is that the last protective institution against the hardships of the world outside - the family itself - becomes the site where

---

* Charles Dickens, *The Pickwick Papers* (New York: The Modern Library, 1962), p. 215. All subsequent references are to this edition of the novel and page numbers are given in the text in parentheses following the quoted passages.

the most hideous aspects of urban poverty are played out.

The brutalizing influence of poverty, its capacity to eat into the primary human relationships is dramatized even more powerfully in Mrs Bayton's death in the fifth chapter of *Oliver Twist*. Dickens first provides the reader with an overview of the locality where the Baytons live:

> The houses on either side were high and large but very old and tenanted by people of the poorest class... A great many of the tenements had shop fronts; but they were fast closed, and mouldering away; only the upper room being inhabited. Some houses which had become insecure from age and decay, were prevented from falling into the streets by huge beams of wood reared against the walls, and firmly planted on the road.... The kennel was stagnant and filthy. The very rats, which here and there lay putrefying in its rottenness, were hideous with famine.*

Inside one of these filthy hovels a young woman has just died of slow starvation. Grief and the sense of injustice have driven the young woman's husband to the brink of madness. The terrified children are crying bitterly. But the person who grips the reader's imagination is the old woman's mother. As Sowerberry, the undertaker, prepares to leave, the old woman totters up to him and speaks for the first time:

> 'She was my daughter, 'said the old woman, nodding her head in the direction of the corpse; and speaking with an idiotic leer...'Lord, lord! Well it *is* strange that I who gave birth to her, and was a woman then, should be alive and merry now, and she lying there so cold and stiff! Lord, Lord! - to think of it; its as good as a play - as good as a play!'

(*OT*, p.83)

This is macabre enough, but we can still hold back the disconcerting force of the passage by seeing it as the raving of a grief-stricken mother. But the "idiotic leer" and the subsequent "chuckles of hideous merriment" are in fact shown to be attempts at propitiating Sowerberry. The old woman's reason for so doing becomes unbearably clear a moment later:

> 'Stop, stop!' said the old woman in a loud whisper. 'Will she be buried tomorrow, or the next day or tonight? I laid her out; and I must walk you know. Send me a large cloak: a good warm one: for it's bitter cold. We should have cake and wine, too, before we go! Never mind; send some bread — only a loaf of bread and a cup of water. Shall we have some bread dear?' she said eagerly: catching the undertaker's coat...

(*OT*, p.83)

---

* Charles Dickens, *Oliver Twist* (Middlesex: Penguin, 1973), p. 81. All subsequent references are to this edition of the novel and page numbers are given in the text in parentheses following the quoted passages.

Dehumanisation can go no further. The old woman's capacity to feel has been completely displaced by her need to eat. Yet for all its ghastliness the old woman's behaviour is not incomprehensible when we remember that she lives in a world where "the very rats are hideous with famine." "Famine," indeed, is the word around which the whole scene is constructed for it is the single decisive fact in the world of which the old woman is an inhabitant. "I say she was starved to death." screams the dead woman's husband, "I never knew how bad she was till the fever came upon her; and then her bones were staring through her skin...I begged for her in the streets:and they sent me to prison. When I came back she was dying; and all the blood in my heart has dried up, for they starved her to death"(*OT*,p.83) . The old woman may be hideous but the society she lives in is scarcely better.

In Dickens' early novels, then, the optimistic representation of poverty (where the most unbearable implications of poverty are sought to be repressed by essentially middleclass strategies of containment) co-exists with a far more frightening portrayal of the poor in which the primary defensive institution against the most demoralising implications of poverty — the family itself — becomes the site for unleashing the most brutal implications of urban poverty.

This alternation between an uninhibited "horrific" expression of urban poverty and the attempt to contain its most frightening implications itself suggests the urgency with which the world of poor imposed itself on the consciousness of liberal, reform-minded individuals. It was Dickens' friend Thomas Carlyle who most clearly articulated the anxiety of a middle class that saw itself engulfed by a discontented and hungry hoard of working men.

> A feeling very generally exists that the condition and disposition of the Working Class is rather an ominous matter at present;that something ought to be said, something ought to be done, in regard to it. And surely at an epoch of history when Chartism numbered by the million and a half, taking nothing by its iron hooped petition,breaks out into brick bats, cheap pikes, and even sputterings of conflagration; such very general feelings cannot be considered unnatural! To us individually this matter appears and has for many years appeared, to be the most ominous of all practical matters; a matter in regard to which if something be not done, something will do itself one day.[11]

The impending social revolution about which Dickens and Carlyle spoke with such apprehension did not, in fact, materialise. According to E.J.Hobsbawm, what saved the British economy from the brink of collapse was the rapid development of her heavy or capital goods industry. Giant enterprises like the iron and steel foundries, the telegraph companies and, above all, the railway not only revealed the limitless possibilities of technological progress but also injected a new dynamism into the economy. The wealth of the world began to flow into England as English capital goods and English technolgy found huge markets all over the globe. Moreover, large scale enterprises such as the railways implied growing job opportunities, higher wages, and better living conditions for the working class. This led to a process of social amelioration and, significantly, the Chartist movement which had brought England to the verge of a working class revolution, died down after 1848, giving way to the respectable trade unionism that was later to become the hallmark of the Labour Party.[12]

The rising standards of living of the post railway generation and the consequent respectabilisation of society implied the increasing marginalisation of the disreputable poor. Unchanging pockets of poverty, however, not only continued to exist through the 1850s and 60s, they also acquired a new subversive significance. This was especially true of London which was increasingly represented as the "world's metropolis" but which, having remained apart from the textile mills and iron foundaries continued to attract hoardes of casual labourers, mendicants, criminals whose outlook and lifestyle were distinctly pre-industrial. As the *Quarterly Review* put it in 1855:

> the most remarkable feature of London life is a class decidedly lower in the social scale than the labourer, and numerically very large — who derive their living from the street ... for the most part, their utmost efforts do little more than maintain them in a state of chronic starvation ... very many have besides their acknowledged calling, another in the background in direct violation of the eighth commandment, and thus by gradations imperceptibly darkening as we advance, we arrive at the classes who are at open war with society, and professedly live by the produce of depredation.[13]

Ghettoised in their slums, characterised as "the sunken sixth" and most frequently as "the residuum," the London poor did not symptomise the "condition of England" or arouse apprehensions of revolution as they did in the world of Dickens' early novels. Rather the very presence in "the world's metropolis" of a pre-industrial, unsettled, "barbaric" people — a "tribe," as the greatest chronicler of the London poor, Henry Mayhew, called them — resonated ironically against the rhetoric of progress so incessantly churned out by the Victorian establishment.

One way in which respectable London sought to bear the burden of its "residuum" was by separating itself physically from the more visible forms of poverty. A major function of the street improvement drives undertaken during the 50s and the 60s was, as Anthony Wohl has suggested, to push back "the sights and smells of the slum," to ensure that they would not be "as intrusive upon the consciousness of the late Victorians as the rookeries of St Giles and Agar Town had been upon the awareness of an earlier generation."[14] It was not of course possible to legally ensure that "the dangerous classes" would not intrude into the respectable areas, but as Geoffrey Best has suggested, "The main duty of the police . . . and the gatekeeper and the watchmen controlling access to private parks, estates, and streets of the West End . . . was to mitigate for the well off the effects of a variously pathetic or threatening daily inundation of poverty."[15]

Official England sought to further reinforce its difference from the "residuum" by its increasing efforts to categorise the latter as a race apart—morally and even biologically incapable of participating in the process of progress. The idea that "long life in slums is accompanied more or less by degeneration of race"[16] did not become a full-fledged theory until the late eighties, but by the sixties the anthropological approach to the problem of the London poor was already beginning to enter official discourse. "It is well established," wrote a Metropolitan Poor Law Inspector in 1868, "that no town-bred boys of the poorer classes, especially those reared in London, ever except in very rare instances, attain the above development of form (4ft. 10½ in. height and 29 in. chest) at the age of 15. A stunted growth is the characteristic of the race."[17] Roebuck, addressing a working class gathering in 1862, complained that the poor and the rich were separated by "distinctions like the differences of race."[18] Octavia Hill, a pioneer in slum improvement schemes, pronounced that the poor had "*inherited* poor constitutions, violent tempers, feeble wills and degraded tendencies."[19] This kind of quasi-racial perspective led directly to the assertion that with their low "cerebral development," the criminal and pauperised classes differed biologically from "the higher nervous natures."[20]

In the official discourse of mid- and late-nineteenth century, then, the relationship between those who participated in "progress" and those who did not was organised as a set of binary oppositions. The "high nervous nature" of the gentleman was posed against the "low cerebral development" of the pauper, the cleanliness and culture of the West End against the squalor and brutality of the East End, the march of civilisation, symbolised by the railways and the broad thoroughfares, against the unchanging sordidness of the slums. The sanctity of the values of progress was thus preserved by the construction of topographical and racial barriers that separated the respectable classes from the "residuum."

These barriers were, however, often under pressure. The "mighty mob" may not have been politically dangerous in the "age of Improvement" but it did threaten civilization in other ways. The cholera epidemic of 1847-48 which swept through all parts of London, for example, was a chilling reminder that the "disease mist" that germinated in the sewers and the cesspools of the slums cut across all barriers of dwelling and class. *Household Words* was only expressing a popular apprehension when it wrote in 1850 :

> I saw from those reeking and pernicious stews the avenging consequences of such Sin issuing forth and penetrating to the highest places. I saw the rich struck down in their strength, and their darling children weakened and withered ... I saw that one miserable wretch that breathed out his poisoned life in the deepest cellar of the most neglected town, but from the surrounding atmosphere some particles of his infection were borne away, charged with heavy retribution on the general guilt.[21]

This idea of infectious disease as something that refuses to recognise the social and racial barriers with which the civilised world sought to preserve its sanctity is not only at the heart of one of Dickens' later novels, it also points to the kind of significance that the world of the poor acquires in Dickens' later works generally. In contrast to the early novels, where the slum had been made to symptomise "the condition of England," to dramatise in all its terrible reality the living condition of a very large mass of people, the slum in Dickens' later novels is significant not because the poverty and brutalisation that it contains is widespread, but because of its potential to symbolically subvert the mid-Victorian confidence in progress. In Dickens' later fiction the slum becomes the repository of a whole range of images, motifs, narrative paradigms (the excremental imagery in *Our Mutual Friend* or the "sensation" plot of *Great Expectations* are just two examples), which point to a cancer gnawing at the heart of "the world's greatest nation" and obliterate easy distinctions between the respectable and the disreputable, the gentleman and the criminal, progress and regression. In what follows I focus on one of Dicken' later novels, *Bleak House* with the hope of examining in somewhat greater detail some of the themes outlined above.

One of the first striking things about Dickens' later novels is that in them poverty is no longer as widespread as it was in a novel like *The Chimes* for example. To be sure, *Dombey and Son* has its Good Mrs. Brown and *Our Mutual Friend* its Betsy Higden. But these characters far from threatening society as Fagin does, for instance, or embodying the terrible situation of a very large number of people, hover at the edges of a society that is increasingly becoming more prosperous and more respectable. On the other hand the very respectabilisation of society, the increasing emphasis on progress, and the real improvement in the condition of the working class after the late forties, gave to the continuing existence of slums a new subversive significance. Thus Mayhew's *London Labour and the London Poor* (1851) stirred the public imagination in a way that Engels' *Condition of the Working Class in England* (1844) could never have done. As Gertrude Himmelfarb comments :

> While England was congratulating itself on 'the moral and material progress' that was so dramatically exhibited in the 'fairy palace' (the Crystal Palace) as cliche had it . . . *London Labour* was giving evidence of quite another England. Mayhew's street folk were not part of the nation celebrated in the Great Exhibition, not even a part of Disraeli's 'two nations,' but rather a primitive 'tribe,' 'folk' or 'race.'[22]

"Outcast London," in other words, could no longer be treated simply as a fact. Juxtaposed against the contemporary rhetoric about progress, the existence of the `residuum' acquired an irony that it did not have in the earlier parts of the nineteenth century.

In *Bleak House*, in fact, Dickens seeks to transform the social topography of London into an "image zone," "a configuration pregnant with tension,"[23] that brings together, through the use of clashing imagery, Dickens' perception of the contradictions inherent in the mid-Victorian confidence in civilization. One way in which Dickens does this is by extending the regressive imagery that had underlain his treatment of the law, to the London poor, and in the process emphasising, like Mayhew, the presence not just of poverty or hunger, but unimaginable primitivism at the heart of the world's greatest nation. Dickens' early novels are not lacking in slum dwellers, but what distinguishes the street urchin Jo in *Bleak House* from even the most brutalised poor in *Oliver Twist* or *The Chimes* is the sheer primitivism of the former's existence. Jo's clothes are like "rank leaves of swampy growth that rotted long ago" (p. 686), a passive analogy which becomes frighteningly animate when Jo fingers his bit of fur cap as though "it were some mangy bird he had caught and was plucking before eating raw" (p.411). The subversive implications of this kind of imagery come into the open in chapter 19 when Dickens brings together Jo, and that ultimate symbol of moral progress, St. Paul's Cathedral, in a dramatic juxtaposition :

> And there he sits munching and gnawing and looking up at the great Cross on the summit of St. Paul's Cathedral, glittering above a red and violet tainted cloud of somke. From the boy's face one might suppose the sacred emblem to be in his eyes, the crowning confusion of a great, confused city. (p. 326)

Held in a relationship of tense simultaneity with the "barbaric" Jo "the sacred symbol" on top St. Paul's cannot retain its inner integrity and becomes transformed instead into "the crowning confusion of a great and confused city."

The official world in *Bleak House* would certainly not share Dickens's perspective on Jo. Jo's existence may be just as real as that of St. Paul's Cathedral, but respectability in *Bleak House* and indeed in mid-Victorian society as a whole demanded increasingly the bracketting away of what *The Fortnightly Review* described as "social, moral and religious anarchy, that is everything excluded by the term civilisation."[24] Henry Mayhew and other socially conscious investigators may have exposed the barbaric conditions of slum dwellers in the age of Improvement, but in the very year of the publication of *London Labour*, G.R. Porter declared in his best selling *Progress of A Nation* that the act of suppressing the sordid realities of "low life" was itself a sign of improvement.

> It is indeed a proof of no slight insignificance, as to the general refinement of manners, that in a work of this nature there would be found an impropriety in describing scenes that were of everyday occurrence formerly.[25]

Porter's sanctimonious tone rings loud and clear in the official world of *Bleak House*. Fashionable society in *Bleak House* has an ideological stake in shutting out anything that problematizes its status as the elite of the world's most civilised nation. Sir Leicester and his circle, Dickens tells us, "have agreed to put a smooth glaze on the world, and to keep down all its realities" (p.211), and when Tulkinghorn responds to Lady Deadlock's inquiries about Hawdon, Sir Leicester is indignant at the mere mention of poverty in his drawing room :

> 'I was directed to his lodging – a miserable poverty stricken place – and I found him dead., You will excuse me Mr. Tulkinghorn,' observes Sir Leicester. 'I think the less said –'
>
> 'Pray Sir Leicester let me hear the story out' (it is my Lady speaking) ... Mr. Tulkinghorn reasserts it by another inclination of his head.
>
> 'Whether by his own hand –'
>
> 'Upon my honour !' cries Sir Leicester, 'Really !' 'Do let me hear the story' says my Lady . . . Sir Leicester's gallantry concedes the point; though he still feels that to bring this sort of squalor among the upper classes is really—really—
>
> (BH pp. 215-16)

Sir Leicester's attitude is symptomatic of official England as a whole. In the world of *Bleak House*, Jo and their likes are treated as, in

Mayhew's expressive phrase, "a proscribed class," a race apart, who are not even strictly speaking citizens of the great British nation, "the government population returns," as Mayhew said of his street folk, "not even number them among the inhabitants of the nation."[26] Thus Jo may have been the only person to have known Hawdon personally, but still his presence in the court inquiring into Hawdon's death is a "terrible depravity."

> 'This won't do gentleman!' says the Coroner, with a melancholy shake of the head.
>
> 'Don't you think you can take his evidence sir?' asks an attentive juryman.
>
> 'Out of the question' says the Coroner, 'You have heard the boy. Can't exactly say won't do you know. We can't take *that* in a court of justice. It's a terrible depravity. Put the boy aside.'
>
> (BH pp. 199-200)

"Put the boy aside" — these four words contain "the one grand recipe — the profound philosophical prescription" (p.203) with which the official world in *Bleak House* deals with the problem of Jo. From the time he is born to the time he dies Jo has always been "moved on," so that his obnoxious presence does not disturb the comfortable world of progress:

> 'This boy,' says the constable, 'although he is repeatedly told to, won't move on -' 'I'm always a moving on, sir,' cries the boy wiping always his grimy tears with his arm. 'I've always been a-moving and a-moving on, since I was born. Where can I possibly move to, sir, more nor I do move!'
>
> 'He won't move on,' says the constable calmly ... 'although he has been repeatedly cautioned, and therefore I'm obliged to take him into custody.'
>
> (BH pp. 319-20)

Jo is moved on, in his own words, "as far as ever I could go" (p. 702). Nevertheless he still infects Esther with a deadly disease before he finds his final refuge in "the berrin' ground." Dickens' delineation of Jo's disease, in fact, incorporates, in the interests of radical fiction, some of the most interesting nuances in the contemporary response to infectious disease. Originating in "alluvial fields and material forests,"[27] travelling through the slums of London to the city as a whole, the epidemics of infectious disease that ravaged mid-Victorian London, had not only suggested connections between "the world's metropolis" and the "miasmic swamps" of "the dark continents," they had also demonstrated, in hard physical terms, that they were, as Dr. Sutherland insisted, after the great cholera epidemic of 1849, "no respecter of classes."[28] The infection that Jo spreads emerges in *Bleak House* as a powerful metaphor under the pressure of which the structuring binaries with which the civilised world seeks to preserve its sanctity collapse completely.

> There is not a drop of Tom's corrupted blood but propagates infection and contagion somewhere. It shall pollute, this very night, the choice stream (in which chemists on analysis would find the genuine nobility) of a Norman house, and his Grace shall not be able to say Nay to the alliance. There is not an atom of Tom's slime, not a cubic inch of any pestilential gas in which he lives, not one obscenity or degradation about him, not an ignorance, not a wickedness, not a brutality of his committing, but shall work its retribution, through every order of society, up to the proudest of the proud, and to the highest of the high.
>
> (p. 683)

This passage is of immense importance not just because it embodies the central principle around which Dickens organises the divergent themes of *Bleak House* but also because it points to the kind of influence that the continuing existence of poverty in the "age of progress," was to exert on the *form* of his later novels. The conflicts present in the above passage, burst in their intensity, the quadrilateral cage of authorial commentary, and find their dynamic expression in a new kind of plot that inexorably brings together "Tom's slime" and "the choice stream ... of a Norman house" and in the process poses a radical challenge to contemporary assumptions about fictional forms appropriate for a scientific and civilised age.

These assumptions emerge with striking clarity in an article in *Westminster Review* attributed by some critics to George Eliot herself.[29] Modern novelists, *The Westminster Review* insisted, should restrict themselves "more and more to the actual and the possible. Our tastes would be offended were they [modern novelists] greatly to overstep these limitations, for a scientific and somewhat sceptical age has no longer the power of believing the marvels which delighted our ruder ancestors." *The Westminster Review* goes on to list the principles of construction appropriate to contemporary fiction:

> The carefully wrought story which details in orderly chronological sequence; which unfolds character according to those laws which experience teaches us to look for as well in the moral as the material world, and which describes outward circumstances in their inexorable certainty yielding to no enchanter's wand.[30]

It is important not to underestimate the strength of an aesthetic based on fine psychological exposition, on careful construction and on the eschewal of the extravagant, for these are clearly the strengths of the novel tradition that stretches back to Jane Austen and looks forward to Henry James. But it is equally important to take cognizance of the ideological foreclosures inherent in what *The Westminster Review* later describes as "realism."[2] For one thing, *The Westminster Review* associates "realism" with the orderly progression of events and a mode of characterisation which draws its authenticity from familiar experience, in short with aesthetic principles which can function only in the stable, relatively homogeneous "civilised world," and indeed, in the context of nineteenth-century England, "realism" began increasingly to mean, among other things, the accurate reflection of what went on in familiar, civilised, middle class society.[31] Significantly the demand that the novel confine itself to the portrayal of "ordinary domestic relationships,"[32] as Fitz James Stephen put it, is made not only by *The Westminster Review*, but also by some of the most influential critics of the fifties and sixties. Thus Sydney Herbert approvingly quoted Guizot's assertion that the chief strength of the English novel lay in its familiarity:

> They are books describing a virtuous domestic life. They do not go to the tragic or the dramatic for interest, but they draw from the simple springs of natural life.[33]

For William Mackay the test of the success of a novel was whether or not its characters were "more real to us than Mr. and Mrs. Jones who live in the next square."[34] In other words, by bracketting away not only the unpredictable but also a whole area of social life where the unpredictable and the uncertain dominate, "realism," in mid-Victorian critical establishment's sense of the term, reinforces at the artistic level, the structural demarcations so essential for the preservation of a single, homogenized, "civilised" world.

Bleak House is not of course the first work of fiction that steps beyond what Fitz James Stephen describes as "the legitimate province of the novel."[35] The Newgate novels of the 30s and early 40s had delved into the lives of slum dwellers and especially of criminals. Still, it is significant that Ainsworth, Bulwer and Dickens had preserved the sanctity of the respectable world by clearly distancing it from the criminal underworld. In *Oliver Twist*, for instance, Dickens had not shied away from the world of Fagin and Sykes or from emphasising the real threat that it poses to civilised life. But in *Oliver Twist* Saffron Hill had been demarcated structurally from the comfortable world of the Brownlows and the Maylies, it being, after all, inconceivable, that Brownlow's respectability may be based on Fagin's wealth or that Rose Maylie might have a lover in Saffron Hill. In any case by the early fifties the Newgate novel had gone out of fashion, relegated, presumably, to the realm of crude romance that had, as *The Westminster Review* said, "delighted our ruder ancestors," and significantly the two novels of Dickens's "middle period," *Dombey and Son* and *David Copperfield*, reflect the general shift towards "realism." "The social and characterological definitiveness of the hero"[36] which Mikhail Bakhtin noted as a characteristic of realism in nineteenth-century Europe as a whole, determines the social space around which Dickens builds *Dombey and Son*. Thus while Dickens is profoundly critical of the values embodied in Dombey, Carker and the rest, the action of *Dombey and Son* is nevertheless confined within the limits of the world that Dombey inhabits. In *Bleak House*, on the other hand, Dickens not only rejects firm centring of the action within a single social space for a syncopated story line that oscillates violently between the extremes of the social spectrum, he also insists on inexorably bringing these extremes together.

In *Bleak House*, Dickens' dissatisfaction with "realism" is based above all on the conviction that the orderly world of "realism" conceals the fractures within the age of Improvement. Accordingly just as Dickens' imagery had subverted any easy confidence in progress, *Bleak House* develops a narrative strategy that radically destabilises the notion of a homogeneous, stable, civilised world. One way in which Dickens does this is by refusing to allow his action to remain for long within a single social space. Chapter 16, for instance, begins with a description of Chesney Wold with its "great drawing room" and its "stately oaks" (p. 271). It moves to the elegant Deadlock town house where "one Mercury in powder, gapes disconsolate at the hall window" (p. 272). At this point Dickens, anticipating the editing techniques of cinema, introduces a sharp "cut," and the comfortable, somewhat languid ambience that surrounds civilised society instantaneously evaporates as the scene moves to Tom all Alone's:

> Jo lives — that is to say Jo has not yet died — in a place known to the like of him by the name of Tom all Alone's. It is a black dilapidated street, avoided by all decent people; where the crazy houses were seized upon, when their decay was far advanced, by some bold vagrants, who after establishing their own possession, took to letting them out in lodgings.
>
> (p. 272)

By shifting rapidly from Chesney Wold to Tom all Alone's in the course of a single, uninterrupted narrative sequence Dickens is not merely stepping beyond "the legitimate province of the novel," he is also defamiliarising the familiar, forcing us to look at the familiar from a new point of view. Such a narrative strategy opens up new possibilities for the kinds of connections that can be plotted in fiction, possibilities which, moreover, challenge the basic assumptions of the realistic novel:

> What connexion can there be, between the place in Lincolnshire, the house in town, the Mercury in powder, and the whereabout of Jo, the outlaw with the broom, who had the distant ray of light upon him when he swept the churchyard step? What connexion can there be between many people in the innumerable histories of this world, who, from opposite sides of great gulfs have nevertheless, been very curiously brought together.
>
> (p. 272)

The plot that involves the slow exposure of precisely such an "impossible" connection, between the glittering Lady Deadlock and the pauperised soldier Hawdon. Lady Deadlock's social position is at the very centre of "the brilliant and distinguished circle" (p. 204) and her life revolves around the elegant Chesney Wold. Her former lover, on the other hand, is not only poor but dies in circumstances that are positively disreputable.

> Poverty had gripped it [the dead Hawdon's room] ... In the corner by the chimney, stand a deal table and a broken desk, a wilderness marked with a rain of ink. In another corner, a ragged old portmanteau on one of the two chairs, serves for cabinet or wardrobe; ... The floor is bare; except that one old mat, trodden to shreds of rope-yarn lies perishing upon the hearth. No curtain veils the darkness of the night, but the discoloured shutters are drawn together; and through the two gaunt holes pierced in them, famine might be staring in —
>
> (p. 188)

Sir Leicester certainly cannot imagine that there might be a connection between this sordid room and the august Chesney Wold. The events that go into the making of the Hawdon-Lady Deadlock plot, however, not only force Sir Leicester to acknowledge the existence of his wife's former lover, they also lead inevitably to Lady Deadlock's death at a pauper's graveyard, whose full repulsiveness emerges in an earlier exchange between her and Jo.

> By many devious ways, reeking with offence of many kinds, they come to the little tunnel of a court, and to the gas lamp (lighted now), and to the iron gate.
>
> 'He was put there,' says Jo, holding to the bars and looking in.
>
> 'Where? O, what a scene of horror!'
>
> 'There!' says Jo, pointing. 'Over Yinder. Among them piles of bones, and close to that kitchen winder! They put him very nigh the top. They was obliged to step upon it to get it in. I could unkiver it for you with my broom, if the gate was open.' (p. 278)

Dickens' decision to locate the climactic moment of the Lady Deadlock-Hawdon plot at the paupers' graveyard is prepared for carefully. Thus even before Dickens has suggested any connection between Lady Deadlock and the place where she ultimately dies, the paupers' graveyard emerges, like the Chancery, as a site where the dominant preoccupations of the novel— the conviction about the coexistence of barbarianism and civilisation in the world's greatest nation, the use of disease as a metaphor that dissolves the barriers between the civilised and the barbaric — are most sharply focussed.

> With houses looking on, on every side, save where a reeking little tunnel of a court gives access to the iron gate — with every reeking villainy of life in action close on death, and every poisonous element of death in action close on life — here, they lower our dear brother down a foot or two: here, to sow him in corruption, to be raised in corruption: an avenging ghost at many a sick bedside: a shameful testimony to future ages, how civilisation and barbarianism walked this boastful island together.

(p. 202)

The significance of the paupers' graveyard as a site where Lady Deadlock's career reaches its denouement lies of course in that it renders dramatic and palpable some of the ideas expressed discursively in the form of authorial commentary. Dickens' insistence on bringing together barbarianism and civilization could not find a more powerful embodiment than in the figure of the splendid Lady Deadlock wading through "the fearful slime" of the paupers' graveyard, the tension of which situation is intensified further when we remember that city burying grounds such as the one described in *Bleak House* actually existed in the mid-Victorian age and that many of Dickens' readers were acquainted with the public exposure of the horrors of "city internments" that appeared so frequently during the 40s and the 50s. Some of these disclosures are worth quoting because they bring out the horrifying reality that lay behind Dickens' somewhat softened descriptions of city burial grounds. According to Dr. Lynch there was a churchyard in St. Bartholomew which was "not more than 10 feet wide by 45 or 50 feet long — it is impracted or stuffed, crammed with dead bodies." In order to reach it one had to wade through "the excrementitious matter flowing down," the families in the vicinity being in the habit of "emptying their chamber pots into this churchyard."[37] And Mrs Signot testified to *The Times* that she had seen "four human heads thrown up."[38] It is only when we realise that in order to reach her former lover's grave Lady Deadlock had to walk through "excrementitious matter," that she might easily have been buried, or rather "stuffed or impracted" among the rotting corpses of paupers, that we can appreciate the violence with which *Bleak House* smashes the ideological, social and topographical barriers with which civilised society seeks to preserve its sanctity.

For Lady Deadlock herself the journey to the terrible place where Hawdon is buried is an act of self recognition. By choosing to die at the paupers' graveyard, with "one creeping round a bar of the iron gate, and seeming to embrace it" (p. 868), Lady Deadlock seems to be silently acknowledging the reality of her relationship with the world of Hawdon, to be coming to terms with that part of her identify that she has always suppressed. Dickens, it would seem, wishes to force Lady Deadlock's recognition on English society as a whole, for it is with the act of bringing to the surface the unacknowledged lower depths of the age of Improvement that *Bleak House* is above all concerned.

The "romantic" or as it came to be known after it had become a rage during the sixties, the "sensation" plot which *Bleak House* pioneers is of major significance to Dickens' subsequent development as a novelist. The more the Victorian establishment sought to push to th realm of the unmentionable, the world of poverty, crime and violence, the greater the violence with which novels like *Little Dorrit, Great Expectations* or *Our Mutual Friend* were to raise it to the surface. Moreover one of the directions that the "sensation" plot began to take from the late sixties is not without relevance to the general themes explored in this volume. The problematisation of the relationship between "civilization" and its degraded "other," which lay at the heart of the "sensation" plot began increasingly to find a new set of correlatives in the "civilised" West and the "pestilential" East. The process by which the zone of poverty and darkness is pushed beyond the seas to the land of "thuggees" and opium, only so that it might be recuperated and made to work its devastation in the heart of respectable England had already begun with Dickens' last (incomplete) novel and it was to go on to *The Heart of Darkness* and beyond.

Notes

1. Quoted in E.J. Hobsbawm, *Industry and Empire* (Middlesex: Penguin, 1973), 95.
2. On the precariousness of the English economy during the first half of the nineteenth century see Hobsbawm, *Industry and Empire* esp. 76-95.
3. Fredrich Engels, *The Condition of the Working Class in England* (Moscow: Progress Publishers, 1977), 63.
4. For a fuller discussion on the relationship between poverty and the early nineteenth century novel see Humphrey House, *The Dickens World* (Oxford: Oxford UP, 1972), 62-68, Gertrude Himmelfarb, *The Idea of Poverty in England in the Early Industrial Age* (London: Faber, 1984), 100-288, and 403-89, Sheila Smith, *The Other Nation:*

The Poor in the English Novels of the 1840s and 1950s (Oxford: The Clarendon P, 1980).
5. Charles Kingsley, *Alton Locke* (London: Dent, 1970) 14 and 101.
6. Quoted in Himmelfarb, *The Idea of Poverty*, 458.
7. Charles Dickens, *The Letters of Charles Dickens* ed. Madeline House and Graham Storey (Oxford: The Clarendon P, 1969) II, 201.
8. Louis Cazamian, *The Social Novel in England, 1830-1850*, tr. M. Fido (London: Routledge and Kegan Paul, 1972) 155-57.
9. Himmelfarb, *Idea of Poverty*, 464, 463, 464.
10. *Idea of Poverty*, 143.
11. T. Carlyle, *Selected Essays* (London: Dent, 1972) 165.
12. On the consolidation of the British economy during the late 1840s see Hobsbawm, *Industry and Empire* esp. 109-34. The mid-Victorian political and social consensus is discussed at length in Geoffrey Best, *Mid-Victorian Britain 1815-1875* (London: Wiedenfield and Nicolson, 1971) esp. 3-22, and Harold Perkin, *The Origins of Modern English Society 1780-1880* (London: Routledge and Kegan Paul, 1969) 270-375.
13. Quoted in Gareth Steadman Jones, *Outcast London* (Oxford: Oxford UP, 1971) 12.
14. Anthony S. Wohl, *The Eternal Slum: Housing and Social Policy in Victorian London* (London: Edward Arnold, 1977) 32 and 28.
15. G. Best, *Mid-Victorian Britain*, 272-73. Hippolyte Taine also observed: "At the gate of St. James' Park is the following notice: 'The park keepers have orders to prevent all beggars from entering the gardens, and all persons in ragged or dirty clothes, or who are not outwardly decent and well behaved." See Hippolyte Taine, *Notes on England*, tr. with an introduction by W.F. Rac (London: Strafar and Co., 1972) 16.
16. See Steadman Jones, *Outcast London*, 128.
17. Quoted in *Outcast London*, 129.
18. Quoted in Unsigned, "Gentleman," *Cornhill Magazine*, Nov. 1862, 327.
19. Quoted in *Outcast London*, 217.
20. Arnold White quoted in *Outcast London*, 223.
21. Unsigned, "A December Vision" *Household Words*, Dec. 14, 1850.
22. Himmelfarb, *Idea of Poverty*, 365.
23. Walter Benjamin, *Illuminations* tr. by Harry Zohn (New York: Harper and Row, 1981) 397.
24. Unsigned, "Civilization and Crime" *Fortnightly Review* 2 (1856): 322.
25. G.R. Porter, *The Progress of the Nation* (London: John Murray, 1851) 681.
26. Henry Mayhew, *The London Labour and the London Poor*, II: 3, and I:1.
27. Phrases such as these were common in contemporary discussions on the origins of cholera. See Asa Briggs, "Cholera and Society in the Nineteenth Century" *Past and Present*, 19 (1961): 76-91.
28. Quoted in "Cholera and Society in the Nineteenth Century," 84.
29. On the authorship of "The Progress of Fiction as An Art Form" *The Westminster Review* (Oct. 1853), see Richard Stang, *The Theory of the Novel in England 1850-*

1870) (London: Routledge and Kegan Paul, 1959) 146.

30. Unsigned, "The Progress of Fiction," *WR*, 343-44. See also J.S. Mill's analysis of the decline of "romance" in England: "Englishmen became more secure both in person and in property. The tide of their existence flowed more smoothly: its course was less habituated to be broken by sudden and violent and sudden shocks. In a word their life became more tranquil — less liable to be disturbed by violent emotions." John Stuart Mill, "Article on French Novels" *Westminister Review*, 25 (July 1836): 308.

31. For more extended discussions of the relationship between realism and the "civilized" middle class world, see Walter C. Phillips, *Dickens, Reade and Collins: Sensational Novelists* (New York: Columbia UP, 1919) 100-28, Kenneth Graham, *English Criticism of the 1865-1900* (Oxford: The Clarendon P, 1965) 21-62, and Winifred Hughes, *The Maniac in The Cellar* (New Jersey: Princeton UP, 1980) 50-55.

32. Fitz James Stephen, "The License of Modern Novelists" *Edinburgh Review* CVII (July 18, 1857): 125.

33. Quoted in Walter Phillips, *Dickens, Reade and Collins*, 102.

34. Quoted in Kenneth Graham, *English Criticism*, 24.

35. Fitz James Stephen, "License of Modern Novelists" 125.

36. Mikhail Bakhtin, *Problems of Dostoyevski's Poetics* ed. and tr. Caryl Emerson (Manchester: Manchester UP, 1984) 101.

37. Dr. Lynch, "Report from the Select Committee of Improvement of Health of Towns: On the Effect of Internments of Bodies in Towns" *Parliamentary Papers* (1842): 160-62.

38. Quoted in *The Times*, September 18, 1848.

4

F.R. Leavis on *Hard Times*

O.P. Grewal

Most academics associated with English studies in India take it as an axiomatic truth that the study of English literature made a powerful positive impact on the Indian sensibility during the nineteenth and early twentieth centuries. The efflorescence of literary activity witnessed in different Indian languages during this period is cited as evidence of the fertilizing effect of our contact with the humanistic values and the liberal outlook embodied in the classics of English literature. That the power-structure of the colonial regime exerted severe distorting pressures on these values is often acknowledged but it is also asserted at the same time that a new ferment was in fact created in the Indian society through the western system of education introduced by the British. The dissemination of literary texts made possible through the expansion of this education, it is claimed, played a major role in the creation of forward-looking and progressive elites and formation of a new sensibility among them. Admittedly, a section of the western educated elements played a seminal role in bringing about an awakening among the masses and encouraging them to come out of the sloth which had overtaken them because of the oppressive and exploitative conditions in which they had been forced to live for centuries. The British rulers, it is conceded, sought to produce through their education system an army of servile Indians who were virtually cut off from the rich cultural traditions of this country and looked to the West for inspiration and guidance, accepting the British rule as a divine dispensation which had brought to them enlightenment, justice and progress and tamed the forces of barbarism and chaos which otherwise would have been rampant. Yet the net result of an exposure of the western educated elites to the ideas and values contained in the great classics of western literature, it is maintained, was quite different in many cases from what had been visualized under the strait-jacket of the cultural policy of the British.

Whatever cultural stamina and creativity there was in the thinking of western educated elites, it did not find an effective expression in the tradition of literary studies which emerged in India. Under the baneful influence of the colonial establishment, even the sturdiest talent active in this field seems to have become a part of the stolid and insipid Victorianism which governed the total environment prevailing in English Departments of most universities in India. During the nineteen thirties and forties, the Scrutiny group of critics led by F.R. Leavis launched an attack on the intellectual vacuousness and cultural obsolescence of literary studies in England and exposed the sterility and inanity of the cultural baggage being exported to the colonies under the sponsorship of agencies like the British Council. But this formidable challenge to the literary establishment in England posed by the Scrutiny critics failed initially to make any impact on scholars in India associated with English studies. The *belles letters* tradition whose triviality was so effectively highlighted by Leavis remained fully entrenched in India in a sanctified form till the fifties. It is only when the decolonising process of our thought and culture started after Independence that the relevance of the dissenting voice of the Scrutiny school was recognised in India.

It has, however, to be kept in mind that in subtler forms, even Leavis carries within his perspective and value-system a conservatism which we shall have to guard against if we want the decolonisation of our thought to grow in strength and become really effective. This task is very difficult because the conservatism which forms an integral part of Leavis' thinking on intellectual and cultural issues is deeply embedded in the sensibility of even those sections of the educated elites in India who have adopted a radical perspective over the years. The two main aspects of this conservatism which can be particularly identified are elitism and a prejudiced view of the social progress which becomes possible through the use of scientific technology.

One of the most negative aspects of the framework of the cultural policy of the colonial regime in India was to insulate the English educated elites from the common masses and prevent their meaningful participation in the creative endeavours of the people. In the absence of an organic and intimate contact with the popular cultural practices, the achievements of the western educated elements in India have seldom attained full vigour and vitality, and their attitude towards the common masses has either been that of contempt and prejudice or at best of condescending patronisation. A major aspect of the debilitating legacy of colonial conditioning of our cultural scene is this hiatus created between the educated elites and the common people. Apart from the elitist trend, the other negative aspect of this legacy is an undue mistrust among the western educated sections in India of the scientific development and the entire process of modernisation of society through the use of machines and technology. A fairly large component of the Indian intelligentsia tends to accept scientific development primarily as a necessary evil and harbours all kinds of melodramatic apprehensions about the harmful impact that technology and science will have on our social and cultural life. In the context of a developing society where rapid and radical social change by increasing productivity and application of new techniques and skills is unavoidable, such inhibitions and fears about scientific development and scientific temper have no justification whatsoever. Both these limiting aspects of the sensibility of the educated middle class in India are present in their stringent form among scholars associated with the study of English literature. Only a sharp realization of the need for liberation from the colonial conditioning in the sensibility of these scholars could enable then to achieve a meaningful participation in the live issues of our time. With all the moral rigour and strenuous purity of dissidence which F.R. Leavis displays in his critical writings, the position he takes on cultural and literary issues carries the weaknesses mentioned above and he affirms his prejudices with extraordinary tenacity and force. Leavis' assumptions about the relationship between the elites and popular culture as also about the basic thrust of historical development in modern times must be critically examined by us from a perspective consonant with the needs and requirements of our developing society. Only after such an exercise can the proper relevance of F.R. Leavis as a figure providing impetus to the process of decolonization of the literary-critical thinking of English studies in India be properly ascertained. What Leavis has said on the strengths and weaknesses of Dickens as a novelist, particularly his reading of *Hard Times* could serve as a basis for such a critical examination.

Leavis had great regard for Dickens' creative genius and yet he was not much impressed by his actual achievement in particular works. He realized quite clearly that by virtue of his natural equipment, Dickens as a writer was very different from the other Victorians like Thackeray and Trollope with whom he had been grossly lumped by the undiscriminating academic critics. For Leavis, Dickens gifted as he was with creative exuberance and a marvellous command over language, belonged not with Thackeray or Trollope but with the poetic dramatists like Shakespeare. He takes note of Dickens' "energy of vision and registration," the "gusto" with which he observes the "humaneness of humanity" and the "vitality that we don't look for in Flaubert."[1] Commenting on his "great command of word, phrase, rhythm and images" he says :

> This comes back to saying that Dickens is a great poet: his endless resource in felicitously varied expression is an extraordinary responsiveness to life. His senses are charged with emotional energy, and his intelligence plays and flashes in the quickest and sharpest perception.[2]

This is a glowing tribute indeed. It might, therefore, look surprising why Dickens should not have qualified for a central position in the great tradition of Leavis' conception. He seems to come so close to the ideal Leavis uses as his standard of Judgment : "a vital capacity for experience, a kind of reverent openness before life, and a marked moral intensity."[3]

The real trouble with Dickens for Leavis is that he is merely a great popular entertainer. He lacks that serious commitment to his art which according to Leavis could serve to bring to an "intense focus" the "unusually developed interest in life" a great writer would invariably have.[4] The result is that as a rule Dickens squanders away his creative energies by writing according to an easy formula, throwing together humour, pathos and melodrama in his large and genial way. In his essay on *Dombey and Son*, first published in 1962, Leavis tells us how there is always a danger in Dickens of "his wonderful vitality" running "too much to repetitiveness or to the cheapnesses and banalities of Victorian popular art." As a public entertainer, he gets a licence for "endless over-worked pathos," for "lush unrealities of high moral insistence" and for "childish elaborations of sensational plot" so that it becomes difficult to respond to the "rhetorical and sentimental art" in the "massive way proposed to us." In the absence of any "unified and unifying imagination," Dickens usually achieves in his works only a "specious totality." The "creative afflatus," we are told, goes "with a moral *elan* that favours neither moral perception nor a grasp of the real."[5] Leavis' impression of the uses to which Dickens ordinarily puts his extraordinary talents could be summed up in these words from that article :

> And so much of the play of Dickens's humorous and comic abundance, even when it issues in the sinister-grotesque, serves the ends of implicit re-assurance : re-assurance that works by implicitly discounting the seriousness of the drama — by intimating that what we have to do with does not, at bottom, make any claim to be the world where the sanctions, conditions and inexorabilities of real life hold without remission.[6]

Thus in Leavis' reading, Dickens the public entertainer, despite his marvellous gifts, rests contented with easy triumphs which would hardly engage or sustain the interest of an adult mind. He feels that Dickens does occasionally allow himself to be controlled by a compelling vision of contemporary civilization, its ethos, its realities, its drives; and then his art becomes distinctively of the superior kind. In this assessment of the positive strength of Dickens' art, too, as we shall see later, there is an over emphasis and misreading, which the literary scholar in India cannot afford to overlook.

Leavis thinks that *Hard Times* is perhaps the only novel where Dickens almost entirely succeeded in overcoming the disabilities he inflicted upon himself as a popular entertainer. "Of all Dickens's works," Leavis maintains, "it is the one that has all the strength of his genius, together with a strength no other of them can show—that of a completely serious work of art."[7] The Dickensian vitality, we are told, is controlled here by a "profound inspiration" and "as he renders his full critical vision" his art achieves "a stamina, a flexibility combined with consistency, and a depth that he seems to have had little credit for."[8] No wonder that *Hard Times* was the only novel of Dickens singled out for comment in *The Great Tradition*. In the first chapter of this book we find Leavis asserting :

> The adult mind doesn't as a rule find in Dickens a challenge to an unusual and sustained seriousness. I can think of only one of his books in which his distinctive creative genius is controlled throughout to a unifying and organizing significance, and that is *Hard Times*, which seems, because of its unusualness and comparatively small scale, to have escaped recognition for the great thing it is.[9]

He feels that here Dickens "is for once possessed by a comprehensive vision, one in which the inhumanities of Victorian civilization are seen as fostered and sanctioned by a hard philosophy, the aggressive formulation of an inhuman spirit."[10] In Leavis' view Dickens has offered a very convincing dramatic embodiment of a major theme and the confutation of utilitarianism by life is conducted with great subtlety. The satiric irony used in dealing with the manifestations of the inhuman spirit as evidenced in his descriptions of Coketown and his treatment of characters like Gradgrind and Bounderby is most effective and it is integrated into the whole scheme of the novel. He is equally effective, according to Leavis, in his treatment of the generous uncalculating spontaneity, the warm flow of life which, according to him, provides the other polarity in the novel, this being represented by Sleary's Horse-riding and Sissy Jupe. Dickens' dramatization of his positives is seen by Leavis as being on the whole free from his usual sentimentality.[11] Only in the case of Stephen Blackpool, Leavis finds some sentimentaliy, but this too does not, in his view, have any serious damaging effect on the novel. Nor do the other limitations of Dickens, limitations visible in his treatment of trade-unionism and the part played by religion in the life of nineteenth century industrial England, detract much from the strength of Dickens' understanding of the realities of the situation. Leavis maintains that "Dickens's understanding of Victorian civilization is adequate for his purpose; the justice and penetration of his criticism are unaffected" by all these limitations.[12].

In his note on *Hard Times* Leavis also draws our attention to the distinctive form of the novel. He suggests that the novel should be viewed as a moral fable where "the intention is peculiarly insistent, so that the representative significance of everything in the fable-character, episode, and so on — is immediately apparent as we read."[13] Once we become aware of the special nature of the form of the moral fable, we shall in Leavis' view, be in a better position to recognize how the characters and episodes have a limited autonomy and are governed by the logic of the basic moral intention which provides symbolic and representative significance to all the different constituents of a coherent whole. As Leavis puts it:

> "The fable is perfect; the symbolic and representative values are inevitable, and, sufficiently plain at once, yield fresh subtleties as the action develops naturally in its convincing historical way."[14]

Leavis' assessment of Dickens' strength as a writer proved to be very influential and brought about a major shift of emphasis in critical opinion. It was now clearly recognized that Dickens' main strength lay in his intense and, in many ways, severely critical response to the unprecedented social conditions created by urbanization and industrialization in England. He lived through a period of accelerated social change and had the necessary intelligence to pierce through the surface details and grasp the essential nature of this change in its totality. He could register the inescapable pressures the rapidly changing social order exerted on the people and the cost in human terms it entailed. Earlier too, critics had sometimes stressed the relevance of Dickens' treatment of some particular social problems in his individuals works — the conditions in schools, the legal system, the problems of orphans and debtors and of the deprived and forlorn in general. But since there was a good deal that was contradictory, or ill-informed, or merely conventional in Dickens' treatment of this or that particular social problem, the real value of his general response to the social reality had not been adequately recognized. Leavis has to be credited with the recognition that Dickens' response was vital primarily in terms of his critical vision of the general movement and ethos of the contemporary industrial and urban civilization, and not in terms of any detachable ideas and opinions he might have had about some subordinate questions. Only Edmund Wilson among the earlier critics had drawn attention to the deep scars on Dickens' sensibility left by his early experiences in Warren's Blacking warehouse as also to the later maladjustments of his personal life and suggested how they had led to his obsessive concern with the criminals and rebels against society. Otherwise, the image of Dickens that prevailed was as it is to be found in Chesterton or Santayana, Orwell or David Cecil. If Dickens is viewed today as a writer who has dramatized, as Raymond Williams suggests, "the haunting isolation; the self-conscious neglect of the damned of the earth; the energy and despair of fixed public appearances, endlessly talking,"[15] if we have learnt to think of him in conjuction with writers like Dostoevsky or Kafka, this has been possible only after the myth of the cheery upholder of Victorian pieties and stimulator of the sound Victorian conscience has been exploded.

Leavis' assessment of Dickens has been influential in another direction too. His emphasis on the poetic and dramatic nature of Dickens' art; his concentration on the texture, imaginative mode, symbolic method in Dickens' works has led to extended studies of his novels focussing on his major symbols, the texture of language and the patterns of coherence achieved by means other than those of the Aristotelian plot or the picaresque narrative mode.

However, many critics, particularly those associated with English studies in India feel today that Leavis' assessment of *Hard Times* amounts to a serious overvaluation. Some sharp comments on Leavis' reading of the novel had been made earlier too by one or two important critics. Holloway had pointed out, for example, in one of his essays how Dickens fails in this novel to deal with utilitarianism "as an ambitious philosophical theory of enlightened and emancipated thinking or of comprehensive social welfare and reform." He feels that Dickens "stood much too near to what he criticized in the novel, for his criticism to reach a fundamental level."[16] It could possibly be argued in reply that since Dickens is writing a satire, he understandably singles out for emphasis only the weaknesses of utilitarianism — its narrow rationality, its naive enthusiasm for statistical data and its tendency to reduce complex human experience to algebraic terms. Dickens was, after all, not refuting utilitarianism as a theory of philosophical enquiry but as a part of what Raymond Williams calls "a social formation," "a practical combination of rationality and exploiting which dominated life in England and which was directly creating new kinds of distress and abuse even while it was reforming many inherited abuses and muddles"[17]. Dickens was concerned with utiltiarianism only to the extent that it had formed a part of the values of people like Bitzer, that "excellent young economist," who had ensured that his mother be shut up in the work-house and considered it a weakness in him to allow her "half a pound of tea a year."[18]

And yet, when we ponder over the mood in which this "social formation" is being attacked by Dickens, we shall discover the real weakness of *Hard Times*. There is a good deal of perspicuity in Dickens' mapping out of the main constituents of the alliance implicit in this social formation and his definition of the quality of their being. Gradgrind as an educationist turned parliamentarian, the blustering and bragging Bounderby as a self-made man and factory owner and the bored and cynical Harthouse as a drifting aristocrat — all are appropriately captured and have a profound representative significance. But is Dickens' presentation searching enough, open-minded enough ? Don't we notice in the satiric irony a breezy expansiveness or, sometimes, a peevishness both of which indicate in different ways how Dickens is trying to skid off the surface of his theme ? He seems to us to have been filled with nervous apprehensions he cannot control or comprehend and tries to dismiss them hastily with a bluff assurance or at times sheer ill temper. This weakness in the quality of Dickens' emotional response could be sensed even in those sections of the novel where the satire is at its strongest, for example, when Dickens is describing the attitudes of Gradgrind and Bounderby by mimicking their idiom and tones. That he chooses the diagrammatic form of the moral fable should, in itself, suggest how he is not patient enough, self-assured enough, to present the hard and inhuman ethos in depth and in detail. His novels like *Dombey and Son, Little Dorrit* and *Our Mutual Friend* are superior achievements precisely because they have both greater perspicuity and resonance with regard to the issues being raised in those works. This weakness in the over-all mood behind *Hard Times* is adequately described by Raymond Williams when he says that *"Hard Times*, in tone and structure, is the work of a man who has `seen through' society, who has found them all out."[19]

If we examine Dickens' treatment of the objects of his satire closely, we could define more sharply some of the blanks in Dickens' understanding of the issues involved and the weaknesses in his response to them. Thus we shall be struck, for example, by a discrepancy between the impact made by the general descriptions of Coketown and the impression left by the individual characters who embody the inhuman spirit active in the township. When we read the description of the piston of steam-engine working "monotonously up and down like the head of an elephant in a state of melancholy madness" (p.27), about that "ugly citadel, where Nature was as strongly bricked out as killing airs and gases were bricked in" (p.65), where "the jail might have been the infirmary, the infirmary might have been the jail, the town-hall might have been either, or both, or anything else" (p.28), we are supposed to experience the appalling nature of the forces ravaging the life of a whole society. However, when Dickens brings in the individual members of the dominating class, we hardly find them formidable. Neither Mr. Gradgrind with his "unbending, utilitarian, matter-of-fact face" (p.9) nor his friend, Mr. Bounderby, "a big, loud man, with a stare, and a metallic laugh" (p.20) would produce in us feelings corresponding to the sensations we experience as we read through the descriptions of drab and disfigured Coketown — a town of "unnatural red and black like the painted face of a savage." (p.27) In his attempt to visualize the essential nature of the ethos of industrial civilization, Dickens was perhaps struck by its crudeness and shallowness as well as its inhumanity. But unfortunately in *Hard Times* his presentation is weakened by the fact that we do not experience the crudeness and inhumanity together. We respond to these two aspects separately, at different levels and in alternating moods.

The weaknesses of the novel are not restricted, however, to the negatives Dickens wants to satrise; they are even more serious in his depiction of the positives. By describing the antithesis between Gradgrindery and Sleary's Horse-riding as a conflict between generous, uncalculating spontaneity and warm flow of life, on the one hand, and the practical and intellectual spirit on the other, Leavis has tried to give a near-Lawrentian turn to the theme of *Hard Times*.[20] But in fact, as pointed out by Holloway, the actual antithesis of Gradgrindery is visualized in the novel in terms of amusement, light fancy, dreams of childhood and flowers of existence, all of which together do not add up to any thing like a challenging alternative to Gradgrindery. We have to agree with Holloway when he says that the main thing Dickens is setting up in opposition to the "hard fact men" does not "seem to be anything even remotely Lawrentian," it is represented by the Slearies "not as vital horsemen but as plain entertainers." "The creed which Dickens champions in the novel, against Grandgrind's," Holloway goes on to add, "seems in the main to be that of "all work and no play makes Jack a dull boy.""[21] This would be sufficiently corroborated from the text. At the beginning of Book I, Chapter 10, for example, we find Dickens saying :

> I entertain a weak idea that the English people are as hardworked as any people upon whom the sun shines. I acknowledge to this ridiculous idiosyncrasy, as a reason why I would give them a little more play. (p.65)

Neither the self-conscious whimsicality of tone nor the phrasing here suggests anything like the assurance and commitment and the deep sense of outrage we find in Lawrence. In an earlier chapter Louisa had complained to her brother Tom :

> I don't know what other girls know. I can't play to you, or sing to you. I can't talk to you so as to lighten your mind, for I never see any amusing sights or read any amusing books that it would be a pleasure or a relief to you to talk about, when you are tired (p.54).

We wonder how Leavis could get an impression of stamina, concentration and depth about a work where the main characters speak at crucial points in such trite language. In the chapter where Gradgrind informs Louisa about Bounderby's desire to marry her, we are told at one point about the "subtle essences of humanity which will elude the utmost cunning of algebra" (p.98), yet the image of fire and of "languid and monotonous smoke" (p.99) to represent those neglected essences does not convince us that Dickens has been able to develop in this novel a clear and effective grasp of the outrage done to an individual when vital needs of his personality are being stultified in the industrial society.

David Hirsch, without raising any question about the ideological justness of Dickens' analysis of industrial civilization in *Hard Times*, challenges Leavis' contention that the novel is an artistic success. He feels that Dickens "does not succeed in converting his very commendable moral intentions into first rate fiction."[22] He takes note of the "superficiality and thinness of Dickens' imagery and symbolism" and argues that Sissy Jupe does not in fact achieve a "potently symbolic role" as claimed by Leavis. For Hirsch she is hardly better than "an ordinary soap-opera heroine."[23] It is indeed rather difficult for many readers to believe how Leavis could see in Sissy an adequate symbol of "life that is lived freely and richly from the deep instinctive and emotional springs."[24] If this continuously fluttering and curtseying figure who so docilely allows herself to be taken up and patronized, who is always hovering in the wings in the Gradgrind household to provide warmth or cushioning whenever it is needed, is not a sentimental figure, we do not know where else sentimentality could be found in Dickens. "Run, Sissy, run, in Heaven's name ! Don't stop for breath." (p.252), we find Dickens writing at one point in the novel. The sloppy sentimentalism of this kind of writing should be unmistakable for any reader who wants to apply his adult mind. Again, even though Mr. Grandgrind is supposed to have undergone some sort of moral regeneration after witnessing the collapse of Louisa's marraige, as soon as he learns that Sissy has providently advised Tom to run away and hide himself with Sleary's travelling circus, he exclaims, "Thank Heaven ! ...he may be got abroad yet" (p.261). And Dickens proceeds to deal in the last few pages of the novel with this factitious problem of getting Tom abroad to Canada or the United States. Obviously, Dickens does not intend here to disturb his readers. He is indulging, on the other hand, in the kind of "reassurance" Leavis himself talks about in the context of his work as a popular entertainer.

The aura of sentimentality surrounding Stephen Blackpool is admitted by Leavis too, though he forgets to mention in this connection Rachael who acts as a guiding star for Stephen Blackpool. It is surprising how Dickens' failure to depict with realism and force the options present before the working class in the industrial city of Coketown should not have, in Leavis' view, any serious damaging effect on the novel. It is understandable that, in his savage mood, Dickens should become aware of the ways in which all institutional activity — trade unionism, different forms of Christianity or the parliamentary debates — should get vitiated by the determining influence of the "social formation" he is satirizing, and it is quite possible that he should not in this mood be able to suggest any specific solution to the appalling problems created by industrialism. But, then at least in his presentation of the problem, he should have shown more resilience and should not have given evidence of succumbing to emotional pressures generated by the situation or seeking easy escapes. It has been rightly observed by critics like Raymond Williams that while Dickens was being forced to develop a sharp awareness on the one hand of the deadly and almost inescapable pressures of the environment created by industrial capitalism, he was also compelled by a generous human impulse to devise at the same time ways of "creative intervention" and transformation. Alienated humanity, no longer able to bear the outrage, asserts itself somehow in these very hopeless conditions and establishes unexpected relationships and "recognitions."[25]

It has, however, to be firmly recognized that this form of transcendence is very often quite unconvincing in Dickens. It seems to be more in the nature of an adjustment than a radical challenge. When confronted with the problems of the industrial working class, Dickens tends to remain satisfied with offering this type of illusory adjustment. Hence the sentimental falsity of Dickens' treatment of the factory workers in Coketown. It isn't so much his belittling the role of trade-unionism in itself as his failure of intelligence and imagination and emotional nerve in depicting the life of the factory workers that introduces a major weakness in the novel. As Raymond Williams tells us in one of his essays : "Dickens both sees the cause and fears the result, holding anxiously and even desperately to those who go on under pressure loving and caring, and trying in his created action to extend their influence."[26] It is this anxiety or desperation overpowering his better judgement that we witness in *Hard Times*.

Leavis' reading of the novel suffers from serious weaknesses which are rooted, as we have tried to show here, in his elitism and his prejudiced view of the developments taking place in English society through the process of industrialization.

Finally, we could mention one more limitation of Leavis' assessment of *Hard Times*, this one having a direct reference to his critical method. Even though Leavis demands maximum concreteness and realization from a work of art, he has a marked preference for measuring the pressures of external social conditions not directly but in terms of their impress on the life of the individuals. He thus has a tendency to distrust the presence in abundance of the details of external life, viewing it as evidence of a moral and imaginative slackness on the part of the writer and a failure on his part to impose tight coherence on his material. This distrust of abundance of characters and description of social environment impels him to view novels and plays as dramatic poems or as moral fables. But a tight coherence apprehended so predominantly in moral psychological terms as is the case with Leavis may fail to take into account multi-layered contradictions of the dialectical process of history. Because of this monistic rigour, there would always be a danger of regarding a selected amount of material as having adequate symbolic and representative significance. Leavis, in fact, sometimes shows evidence of ignoring the need for even psychological complexity. At any rate, he has a marked preference for describing literary works in terms of certain general moral themes. It is his distrust of unnecessary abundance that makes him admire *Hard Times* because of its tight coherence. And it is for this reason too that he fails to concentrate on the weakness in the psychological make-up of the the characters, particularly in those scenes where the characters are overtaken by a sense of crisis. Nor does he show any adequate realization of the inadequacy of the symbols being used by Dickens for representing the full complexity of historical reality. The concepts of "inevitability" and "naturalness" he invokes in describing the form of the moral fable do not take into account, at least not sufficiently, the dialectics of history, and not even the logic of growth of the personality of an individual human being.

Note

1. F.R. Leavis, *The Great Tradition*, Penguin Books, Harmondsworth, 1962, pp. 29, 258, 270.
2. Ibid., p. 272.
3. Ibid., p. 17.
4. Ibid., p. 17.
5. F.R. Leavis, 'Dombey and Son', Sewanee Review, LXX, 2, Spring 1962, pp. 178, 191. The essay has been reprinted in a revised form in *Dickens the Novelist* by F.R. Leavis and Q.D. Leavis, Chatto and Windus, London, 1970.
6. Ibid., pp. 194-195.
7. The *Great Tradition*, p. 249.
8. Ibid., pp. 250, 251.
9. Ibid., p. 29.
10. Ibid., p. 250.
11. Ibid., p. 258.
12. Ibid., p. 271.
13. Ibid., p. 250.
14. Ibid., p. 30.
15. Raymond Williams, *The English Novel From Dickens to Lawrence*, Chatto and Windus, London, 1970, p. 49.
16. John Holloway, 'Hard Times : A History and A Criticism,' in *Dickens and the Twentieth Century*, ed. Gross and Pearson, Routledge and Kegan Paul, London, paperback edition 1966, pp. 159, 166.
17. Raymond Williams, 'Dickens and Social Ideas,' *Sociology of Literature and Drama*, ed. Elizabeth and Tom Burns, Penguin Hammondsworth, 1973, p. 340.
18. Charles Dickens, *Hard Times*, Doubleday and Company, New York, paperback edition 1959, p. 113.
    In the case of all further quotations from the text of the novel, the page numbers will be indicated in parentheses immediately following the portions of the text cited in the paper.
19. Raymond Williams, *Culture and Society*, Chatto and Windus, London, 1959, p. 96.
20. *The Great Tradition*, p. 252.
21. *Dickens and the Twentieth Century*, p., 168.
22. David H. Hirsch, 'Hard Times and F.R. Leavis', *Criticism*, VI. 1, Winter 1964, p. 2.
23. Ibid., pp. 3, 4, 5,.
24. *The Great Tradition*, p. 254.
25. *The English Novel*, pp. 33, 48.
26. *Sociology of Literature and Drama*, pp. 342-43.

5

'The Wings of the Dove: "not knowing, but only guessing"'

Kumkum Sangari

> ...the value I wished most to render and the effect I wished most to produce were precisely those of *our not knowing, of society's not knowing, but only guessing and suspecting and trying to ignore*, what "goes on" irreconcileably, subversively, beneath the vast smug surface.
>
> Henry James, Preface to *The Princess Casamassima*

> The text may, it is admitted, stitch the viewer or reader into position in certain ways; it may offer the subject specific positions of intelligibility; it may operate to prefer certain readings above others. What it cannot do, it is argued, is *guarantee* them.
>
> Tony Bennett, "Text and History"

How does the late Jamesian text 'position' its reader and transform each critic writing on it into a highly individual and sensitive register 'open' to the multiple possibilities inscribed in the narrative? The famous variability of the late Jamesian text, its polysemic penumbra is indeed crucial in situating the reader. This is frequently recognized in studies which locate the text-reader relation as a lucid transaction or as a willing suspension of belief: the reader postulated by the text must in effect promise not to elicit any kind of self confirmation from the text, whether cultural, moral or epistemological.[1] The complex `writerly' readings of James' opacity and fecundity which privilege form and celebrate the plurality of meaning are based on a notion of an auto-referential or self-reflexive literary text which anticipates both the way it will be read and the interpretations it will generate. They opt for "a total relativism" towards the text and a "scepticism towards any reconstruction of the plane of reference" based on a neo-Jamesian identification of the "vulgar" with the "literal" and of the "criminal" with the univocal.[2] In a curious circular fashion the actual reading of the text becomes almost identical with the reader postulated by the text. Such readings exemplify the persuasive power of the late Jamesian text insofar as they come to occupy the collusive reader positions 'formally' prefered by the text. Ultimately, however, the notions of polysemy, difficulty and inaccessibility central to modernist narratives have to be unpacked not in the formal but in the cultural sphere. Epistemological difficulties are not universal — they have specifiable contours and historical locales.

My intention is not to resurrect the late Jamesian text as an essential object but to argue for its sociality and historical 'density', and to show that the cognitive relation it prefers and establishes is produced by and in turn produces a social relation. Both the text's potential for re-interpretation and the difficulty of fixing meaning need to be seen as part of a social transaction involving class, politics and ideology. Neither the fecundity of the late Jamesian text nor the way in which it seeks to position the reader in relation to itself is value free. Both are constrained by their specific ideological character which underwrites the cognitive mode they try to establish. The generative matrix (textual, formal and social) of the text's polysemy which both enables and encourages the production and/or proliferation of meaning simultaneously determines the ideological limits of the plurality of the text. To say this is to *frame* both the late Jamesian text as a site for the production of meaning and the generative activity of the reader it implies, to argue that the text encodes the *conditions* of its re-interpretability, to claim that the *sanction* for a particular mode of plurality is to be found within the given historical moments of the text's production and consumption (which do not remain identical), and so to acknowledge the possibility of 'openness' as being a form of enclosure.

In *The Wings of the Dove* the presence of two broadly different competing epistemologies, the 'realist' and the 'modernist,' creates the generative matrix of the text's plurality which surfaces and flourishes within a conflictive historical moment and so offers a range of "interpretative *temptations*."[3] The polysemy of the text is generated by the structures of surrogacy which unsettle conventions of character and morality only to replace them with other modes of auhority, by the gathering intimacy of the narrator with Merton Densher which signifies the emergence of a corporate consciousness, by the secrecy which underlies the weight given by characters and narrator to the unspoken and by the structure of the text to the unshown, and by the syntactical uncertainty which depends upon and as well as 'replays' the semantic difficulty so produced. The text is both intentional and performative. It is intentional because it is a mode of address which attempts to place the reader in a preferred 'univocal' position *from* which multiple interpretations are possible. The intention of the text is not stated but performed, indeed the enacted or enactive pluralism of the text can itself be taken as the code of its unstated intention which consists in fixing the reader not to a single interpretation but to a *way* of seeing. The factors responsible for the text's polysemy instal "not knowing, but only guessing" as a primary value which in turn shuffles the reader into place, 'regularizes' plurality and so helps to institute *undecidability as a cognitive mode*.

Even on a bare reading of the text the question of the distribution of guilt and responsibility in *The Wings of the Dove* comes to revolve around "the *similarity of the different*" and the "possibility that *the ostensibly different is actually the same*."[4] *All* the major characters — Kate Croy, Merton Densher, Susan Stringham, Maud Lowder, Sir Luke and Milly Theale herself — *urge* the conspiracy along because it fits in various ways with their own designs. Guilt and responsibility mesh with innocence and victimization in the relationships of the protagonists. The debased and materialist Kate is also the aspiring individual trapped in sordid circumstances not of her own making. Both Milly and Maud Lowder, the American princess and the Brittania of the Market Place, manoeuver people and relationships through the power of their money. Both Lord Mark and Densher, the impoverished aristocrat and the penniless journalist, are drawn to Milly's wealthy charm. Further Densher does not simply shift his allegiance from Kate to Milly: he contains within himself the possibilities of *both* women *throughout* the novel. Not only is his apparent rejection of the one and the embrace of the other ambivalent, but the very qualities Kate and Milly embody are fraught with grim similarity. Kate is the social being with a "talent for life," a desire for love and wealth to fulfil her potential, a dominating personality and an uncompromising sense of "reality." Milly is the weak, passive, sensitive heiress, who seeks "life" so as to actualize the potential liberty which inheres in her wealth; in seeking "life" she is prone to self deception. If Kate is the "worker" then Milly is willing to be "worked." Her victimization is assisted by qualities within herself. And yet *both* Kate and Milly accept and enact the roles and self images offered to them.[5] Kate becomes the family pawn who will in the process of redeeming her family's fortune somehow also find something for herself. Milly is glad to be named, to be called a "dove": she will be graceful, benevolent and vulnerable; she will accept domination if in return she can find something for herself. Both the "selfish" and the "selfless" are at one and the same time the "workers" and the "worked."

The plastic Densher slides easily into these enveloping structures of surrogacy in which the underlying grid of similarity between various characters blurs the nature of the confrontations and develops shifting and reinterpretable patterns of conflict and affinity. Densher takes on complementary roles with Kate and Milly insofar as each woman reflects his own potential. He behaves towards Kate as she would towards him; his behaviour towards Milly is almost a reflection of her own towards him. With Kate he speaks the language of hard cash transactions, he strikes bargains, he demands returns. Money as he sees it in relation to Kate is both desirable and inevitably soiled. With Milly he functions through the passive channels of perception and retrospection. His willed self-deception about the nature of his relationship with her is an exact replica of her self-deception regarding his relation with her. Milly's money remains pure, indeed it seems to Densher to be a perfect culmination of and "as fairly giving poetry" to her "life."[6] Yet it is Densher who has embraced the equivocal analogy between Milly's wealth, its power and her dovelike qualities. The dove in Milly combines the softness of beneficence with the hardness of power. The color of the priceless pearls she wears at her party in Venice blends with the color of the dove into a soft radiance which veils but is synonymous with the glitter of her wealth. The chain "wound twice" (2:p.217) around her neck faintly implies entrapment, insinuates against the free flight of the dove. Densher's comparison of this free flight of the dove to the power of wealth implicates him in the simultaneous freedom and bondage of the dove. Just as Kate and Densher state their plan unambiguously for the first time, Milly sends "across towards them in response all the candour of her smile, the lustre of her pearls, the value of her life, the essence of her wealth" (2:p.229) — the value of her life at this moment lies, however, in the value she can bequeath with her death. The same symbol discloses the menace of the dove and also instantaneously idealizes it : Milly is both corrupter and victimized, Kate and Densher are both conspirators and abjects cornered into desire by the power of money. For Kate money is an escape from vulgarity, she acknowledges her guilt. Milly's money deviously takes her beyond guilt : death makes her sacrosanct, "saves" her. Her true expansion comes after death in a symbolic realm. She simultaneously relinquishes wealth and excercises power, a power which intensifies Densher's con-

> words, that he should never, never know what had been in Milly's letter.... The part of it missed for ever was the turn she would have given her act. That turn had possibilities that, *somehow*, by wondering about them, his imagination had extraordinarily filled out and refined. It had made of them a revelation the loss of which was *like the sight of a priceless pearl cast before his eyes - his pledge given not to save it - into the fathomless sea, or rather even it was like* the sacrifice of something sentient and throbbing, *something that*, for the spiritual ear, *might have been* audible as a faint, far wail. This was the sound that he cherished when alone in the stillness of his rooms. He sought and guarded the stillness, so that it *might* prevail there till the inevitable sounds of life, *once more, comparatively* coarse and harsh, should smother and deaden it - *doubtless* by the same process with which they would officiously heal the ache in his soul that was *somehow* one with it.
>
> (2:p.395-96; my emphasis)

The narrator and Densher are as one both in their paternalism, and in their desire to consecrate the sense of loss in the stillness of memory — that realm where imagined possibility subdues the deadening "sounds of life". The narrator joins in the pledge of not redeeming the "pearl" i.e. not revealing the contents of Milly's letter — to Kate, to Densher, to the reader, and by implication to himself.

The difficulty of this passage lies in disentangling the analogies, the modifying words, the parenthetical and qualifying phrases (see my italics) which belong to Densher from those which belong to the narrator. The discretion and delicacy, the hesitation and hypothesis, with which the narrator "handles" Densher's experience is an index of their joined sensibility and style which in turn indicates the preferred attitude to the reader — not knowing, not probing, only guessing. The sentence structures incorporate various hypothetical dimensions of time : prescience and retrospection, the definite past and the indefinite past, the present moment and the indefinable present, the determined future and the indeterminable or undetermined future — all coexist in the combined consciousness of narrator, character and reader. In this way James establishes an alternate and more expansive time scale in which *uncertainty becomes the principle of expansion* — uncertainty blurs the edges of simple, sequential, ascertainable time and so expands it. The stylistic fiat of the narrator is to offer description as conjecture. The simultaneity with which a series of conjectures can be held and pursued is the synchronous stylistic proposition that he holds out to the reader. This betokens not so much a break with causality as a *silencing* interrogation of causality so that sequential thought appears to be both vulgar and inaccurate.

James can "work" this in formal terms because of his contradictory use of and placement between 'realism' and 'modernism' : the modernist dislocations of the text are undergirded, at least in one significant way, by the "unifying" ideology of realism. Broadly speaking the realist novel depends on an apparent settlement between narrator and reader which claims a more or less stable and shared epistemology, while the modernist novel openly contracts to unsettle or destabilize the reader's way of knowing. In *The Wings of the Dove* the narrator is able to share his *hesitation* to fix meaning and morality with the reader in roughly the same way as the omniscient narrators of the realist novel share their knowledge and moral authority. The narrator's presence, marked in the text by the occasional use of "we" and "our," still retains some control and authority,[8] but he offers instead 'moral' assurance in uncertainty. On the one hand narrator and reader are still aligned as in the realist novel, on the other hand the partial break with realism allows the text to instal the reader in a new position, the position from which the text is 'fully' intelligible i.e. the tolerance of the vague and the acceptance of polysemy. Tentativeness and undecidability become the authoritative measure of sensitivity, and so the gauge of a 'higher' morality. The text demands a 'voluntary' (as befits capitalist ideology) renunciation of certainty. Certainty is gross, a vulgar arrest of the fullness of speculation, something which can do only partial justice to reality, and can indicate only a qualitatively inferior reality. The hesitation and uncertainty appear to knit the text itself into a dense, textured, enclosing medium which offers to envelop the reader in another kind of security, and to replace the satisfaction that the closures of the realist novel provide. The narrator does not openly exhort or enlist the reader through the direct explanation and evaluation of character or event. He hesitates openly, displays his stammering lack of omniscience, avoids his 'responsibility' to retail the 'real' events of the story. Yet he manages to maintain a certain 'moral' consensus or accord with the reader : both can share, or rather the reader can come to share with the narrator, a humane and finely discriminating intelligence which depends upon and is produced by uncertainty. Uncertainty becomes both test and guarantor of the quality of such an intelligence. In this way the reader is constituted as simultaneously affiliated to the narrator (at least along an implicit axis of value) as well as an autonomous re/constructor of meaning. The reader can be both a complicit consumer of the text and also a producer of the text alert to its variability.

Undecidability is the upshot of James' own ideological position which is entangled in and encashes two simultaneously present and conflicting epistemologies. Not only does the entanglement engender flation of the spiritual with the material and imprisons him in memory. It is the passive Milly, too generous to confront Densher, who in the final analysis takes her revenge. The power of her wealth is the wedge which splits the relationship of Kate and Densher, her bequest calculably drives them apart. Her excercise of power is all the more effective for being covert. It is Kate, despite all her planning and plotting, who "lets off" Densher with more charity, and who is finally both undeceived and undeceiving. Densher duplicates Milly's tactics in the end, he too uses the power of wealth and the shield of virtue. In a sense he betrays both women : the active worldly principle is negated by his acceptance of the passive role, the passive "transcendental" principle is negated by his guilt, his responsibility, his continuous aggression. But in a fundamental sense the text makes it difficult to maintain the opposition or even distinguish between the two.

Even as the narrative complicates the 'realistic' deciphering of motives and attitudes, the conclusion seems to put the burden of duplicity on Kate largely through the narrator's connivance with Densher. The narrator is increasingly involved and implicated in the very acts of Densher's perception, gradually pervades his consciousness, further confounding the issues of guilt and responsibility.[7] Like Densher's complicity with Kate, the narrator's complicity with Densher is established early in the novel. The instances of Densher's easy compliance with the growing 'plot' are too numerous to retail, but it would be illuminating to look at a few examples of the way his consciousness blends with the narrator's. When Densher returns from America, Milly, a casual acquaintance, is fast becoming a question mark in his mind. He thinks of her already in terms of use (as a "convenience") and of premonition. Milly "popping up in his absence, occupied - he couldn't have said quite why he felt it - more of the foreground than one would have expected her in advance to find clear" (2:p.14). The use of "one" instead of an unambiguous "he" welds Densher's premonitory unrationalized fear and desire with an authorial foreboding which must stem from the foreknowledge of a predetermined "plot." Later Densher knows he is enjoying Milly's "consideration on a perfectly false footing," "soothing" though it is, but feels it would be as indelicate to "challenge her as to leave her deluded" (2:pp.76-77). Besides, that might also mean a "betrayal" of Kate. The fluid prevarication of the narrator assists Densher's prevarication :

> It wouldn't really have taken much more to make him wonder if he hadn't before him one of those rare cases of exaltation - food for fiction, food for poetry - in which a man's fortune with the woman who doesn't care for him is positively promoted by the woman who does. (2:p.81)

The woman in this context could be either Kate, secretly engaged to Densher, or Milly, who likes him and thinks Kate does not.

Later, on his return to London his attitude to the dying Milly is strange :

> He had taken with himself on leaving Venice the resolution to regard Milly as already dead to him - that being, for his spirit the only thinkable way to pass the time of waiting.
>
> (2:p.339)

In the rest of this passage the narrator does not qualify Densher's attitude but its success, which it seems is only partial. The narrator sees it as only natural that Densher should desire both to transfigure Milly and to "ignore" her "consciousness, tortured ...crucified by its pain." This is after all structurally on par with the text's own omission of the last crucial confrontation between Densher and Milly in Venice. In the final scene the hard choice is once again to be Kate's whereas Densher is to have the luxury of inaction. She cannot have the money except through him, and he will only renounce it through her. According to the terms of his bargain, he can remain evasive : it is to be Kate's renunciation or Kate's responsibility. She is both to possess and to exorcise the taint of the money. Whereas Kate is defined and condemned by her actions, Densher's inaction blurs the edges of his guilt. Repeated justifications for his passivity are developed sometimes by him and sometimes with the narrator's help. As an accomplice who has extracted his physical due from Kate, Densher's bid for integrity must have some moral leverage before the reader can make a double judgement by which he is forgiven and she is not. The ground for such judgement is eroded by the narrator who becomes Densher's accomplice, slips into subterfuge about him, and technically condones his behaviour even as the narrative provides contrary evidence. The "moral" solution of the narrator resolves into "doing nothing" to facilitate conventional moral judgement for the reader.

The climactic moment in the narrator's relation with Densher comes near the end of the novel. After the burning of Milly's unread letter there is an expanse of things left unsaid between Kate and Densher. Densher has an added awareness of how "while the days melted, something rare went with them" :

> He kept it back *like* a favorite pang; left it behind him, *so to say*, when he went out, but came home again *the sooner* for the certainty of finding it there. Then he took it out of its sacred corner and its soft wrappings; he undid them one by one, handling them, *handling it, as a father, baffled and tender, might handle a maimed child*.... Then he took to himself at such hours, *in other*

our own fictions — ending our search for the truth, strangely enough, where James' characters so often begin : in the realm of metaphor.

Indeed the more susceptible we are to the reading of any novel — the more we characteristically surrender to the realities that words create, the more emotionally rich, if sometimes disquieting, our reading of the late James must be.[16]

James' contradictory placement between a 'realist' and 'modernist' epistemology reveals itself not just in the structures of surrogacy or in the linguistic and syntactical elaboration of the style but is also inscribed in the structural and structuring secrecy of the text. Even a hasty account shows the polysemy of the text to be produced as much by its stylistic properties as by its 'plot' : by *both* its base and its superstructure to use a convenient if not entirely accurate analogy. On the one hand the text presents a popular melodramatic Victorian plot of greed, corruption, conspiracy, betrayal and death. On the other hand it constructs itself around the cogitations, speculations, and speculation on the speculations of the five centres of consciousness (including Susan Stringham and the narrator). An intricate, enormous superstructure is created from the activity of these combined consciousnesses which *guess* and build webs of possibility and conjecture out of the *unspoken*.[17] Their combined activity refines, sublimates, evades or just ignores the facts of materiality, wealth, sexuality, pain and death on which the plot is based. But these threatening 'facts' have to be *there* in order to be elided. It is the consistent presence and suppression of sordid fact as well as the formal emphasis on conjecture which *together* engender the variable text and constitute a generative matrix for plural meaning/reading. The facts and scenes pushed aside or omitted — the 'crime' of Kate's father, Kate in Densher's room, Milly on her deathbed, the origin of her wealth, the content of her letter, the nature of her disease — become by virtue of their absence the determining centre of the work. This absence, continually indicated, is what *enables* the activity of the individual consciousness and assists in the attendant dilation of time — or the spread into the unquantifiable and the uncertain. To use James' own phrase - "the margin floods the text."

There is an intrinsic structural relation in the text between the superstructure of the consciousness and its basis in plain textual and social facts. If it weren't for the crude almost exaggerated plot there would be nothing to secure and ballast, or to make sensible and palatable, the working of the consciousness and prevent it from becoming either arbitrary or insubstantial. *Because* the factual basis is gross for James the superstructure needs to be refined, because the material foundation is powerful and determining it needs to be supressed. Because social facts are 'real' and inevitable the superstructure needs a utopian dimension. The subtle and refined superstructure of the consciousness cannot really escape its material foundation, so James develops a structural mode which discovers and builds on a tangent, rather than on the contradictions it both conceals and uncovers. And in so doing he begins to disturb its actual foundation in fact e.g. the "innocence" of Densher and the guilt of Kate. Transgressing conventional realism, he does not move towards a final unveiling in which the secrets of the narrative are disclosed. The burning of the unopened letter is literally and symbolically[18] the killing of the motive and victory of guesswork. If the letter is a sign of the process by which money is transferred, acquired, and inherited, then burning it represents an attempt to repress, even destroy, the transactive character of money. Kate is vulgar in opening the second letter, because she is ready to name the "sum," she breaks the rules of the not knowing game, the game Densher will continue to play. In effect the rarefied superstructure begins in willed and wilful fashion to question its basis in factuality, and in turn, the ugly dimensions of the suppressed base and the submerged links between its components (e.g. wealth and sexuality) constantly threaten to engulf the rarefied superstructure of the consciousness. Thus Densher's passion for Kate is a bargain which displays an equivalence between sexuality and money — the one in return for the other. After Kate's visit to his rooms has converted "luminous conception into an historic truth" (2:p.236) Densher's fulfilment communicates itself retrospectively :

> The force of the engagement, the *quantity of the article to be supplied*, the *special solidity of the contract*, the way, above all, as a *service* for which *the price named* by him had been magnificently *paid*, his equivalent office was to take effect - such *items* might well fill his consciousness when there was nothing from outside to interfere. Never was a consciousness more rounded and fastened down over what *filled* it; which is precisely what we have spoken of as, in its degree, *the oppressiqon of success*, the somewhat *chilled state* - tending to the solitary - *of supreme recognition*. If it was slightly awful to feel so justified, this way by *the loss of the warmth of the element of mystery*. The *lucid reigned instead* of it, and it was into the lucid that he sat and stared.

(2:p.237-38; my emphasis)

The conflation of money and sexuality, of commercial success with oppression, of satiety with lucidity, and of lucidity with loss tell their own story, which in part is retold in the text's transaction with the reader. The material and social base cannot but invade the personal relationships which are the content[19] and the catalyst of the individual consciousness, both its nourishment and the reason for its activity. It is plural meaning but it allows him to function as author in determinate ways predicated on the shared epistemology of the realist narrative. Because James is unwilling to forego the cohesive power of an individualism which can 'authorize' and legitimate perspective or point of view, and which can bracket the proliferation of meaning by impressing a single and singular vision on the text, his modernist 'authorization' of plurality is at one level grounded on the apparently stable epistemological compact of realism. In this sense too the text offers only a single subject position[9] which has, however, the capacity to generate different interpretative strategies and various interpretations.

The formal complexity of the late Jamesian text which immediately enlists both the deciphering abilities of the reader/critic as well as his/her tolerance of plural meaning thus expresses both an ideology and a social relation rooted in a particular evaluation of the 'real'. Not only is the "renunciation" of certainty itself an ideological position, it both signifies and requests a willingness to entertain the 'real' as subject to endless ramification and qualification. In formal terms it involves the tacit acceptance of a constant play of meaning albeit still framed by certain forms of authority. A large number of interpretations are in order as long as undecidability as a cognitive mode and its underlying assumptions are not challenged. The accomodation to uncertainty as a principle can save both reader and critic (like Densher) from the tarnish of an unmediated reality, and can guarantee the necessity of his or her own mediation. The critic especially is constituted as a mediator who will assist the reader to gain maximum value (of variability) from the text. And the critic can scarcely extract this maximum from the late Jamesian text unless she or he is willing to go along with its values. Margaret Walters goes even further when she says of *The Awkward Age* that unless the reader accepts the novel's terms and is complicit with both its style and values he/she cannot understand or even make sense of it.[10]

In this context the 'willing' readers and critics of James' later work contrast quite sharply with the 'unwilling' readers and critics. The fact that the unwilling critics were often his own contemporaries shows the different expectations of, and dramatizes the gap between critics schooled on the so-called verities of realism from those who have matured on the fractures of modernism. In 1902 J.P. Mowbray complains that James never arrives at the story in *The Wings of the Dove*:

> How indeed can he, when he is himself the story and has come to believe that the constructive or co-ordinating ability to deal with material is of less account than the exhibition of a superb dexterity in keeping the material on the air....

His generous belief that his reader is gifted not only with agility but with a supernatural acumen to discover what he means without his saying it, is not as preposterous as his confidence that the reader will understand it when he does say it, and both these amiable qualities of the author sink into insignificance by the side of the superhuman faith that the reader will think it worth saying when he has said it.[11]

F.M. Colby ascribes the linguistic "obscurity" of the novel to "self-indulgence," and another anonymous reviewer in 1903 who finds the style and syntax of the novel "irritating" concludes charitably with a gesture towards the advent of an adversary modernism :

> After all, this kind of writing, crabbed, finicking, tedious in its struggle to be exact, intolerable when it tries, so to say, to be exact about nothing, marks a strong reaction against the kind that prevailed until twenty years ago or even later.[12]

In 1905 Tom Masson rewrites a nursery rhyme in James' idiom of parenthesis and overqualification :

> Perhaps it was providential, and yet it seemed to come, in the sequence of events, wholly without vagueness or sense of any obscurity, that is to say, quite naturally, without forethought, or design, or shall I say premeditation ? that the girl Mary, among other nameless characteristics, doubtless alien and beside the question, so to speak, had, at the time, though it were vain to specify the precise hour or moment, this being a matter of debatable chronology, a curious illustration of nature's spend-thrift energies, namely — a lamb.[13]

In 1923 Vernon Lee does not object to the fact that James' style requires a special kind of attentiveness which forces a reader "to be an intellectual, as distinguished from an impulsive or *imageful* person;" but Stephen Spender, for whom James' style is the upshot of his snobbery and conservatism, remarks more acerbically in 1935 that "the privilege the reader is offered is to become Henry James."[14] Despite the occasional rumbling of discontent,[15] in recent years, the willing critic, proficient in making vital `modernist' commitment to uncertainty is more than ready to `surrender' to James' style. Thus Ralf Norrman believes that avoiding both faith and disbelief, "we should stay in the Jamesian thematic mainstream of doubt, vacillation, hesitation and uncertainty," and Ruth Bernard Yeazell votes for a similar "susceptible" reader :

> For like the characters, we too are continuously forced to hover somewhere between ignorance and full knowledge, to struggle with intimations and possibilities which make themselves but obliquely felt. The late style demands that at every point we sense more than we are yet able to articulate; only gradually do we grow fully conscious of our own subliminal guesses.
>
> And in guessing at the facts, in trying to make conscious and explicit all that the characters themselves fear to think and speak, we may conclude by writing

lusion with Densher is not an instance of authorial bad faith but a modus operandi for transforming the individual consciousness so described into a *collective* one. An ideological collectivity of characters, narrator and potentially the reader is posited through the successive alliances the isolated individual (Densher) is seen to make with the narrator's authority and with 'femaleness' (Milly).

The surface dialogy of the text in which different centres of consciousness address each other is subsumed under the broad ideological monolith of a bourgeois consciousness — a cohesive medium punctuated by its own compulsive self-reflexivity. And this 'corporate' consciousness (as befits the ideology of late capitalism)[22] is also based on the in-corporation of 'femaleness'. The cultural definition of 'femaleness' in the nineteenth century is predicated on and indicated chiefly a mode of social being, elicits its subjective 'depth' from the sexual division of labour and the split between public and private spheres. The product of a specific set of social relations, 'female subjectivity,' both pliable in its social formation and pristine in its enforced isolation from the public world is a prime medium through which the formation of a higher, introspective bourgeois consciousness can be enacted.[23] Milly's greater freedom as an American girl/heiress also ironically accounts for her greater pliancy. At one level the feminization of Densher, for whom "plasticity" has always been "within limits... a mode of life like another — certainly better than some" (2:p.182), is completed only with the final transaction which occurs behind the burned letter — the absorption of Milly's 'femaleness' which is both enshrined as unfulfillable potential and "reworked" through memory, thoroughly internalized and individualized. Milly's femaleness, qua her subjectivity, is of greater 'value' than her money, exactly as the burned letter is of more value than the letter from her lawyers. The "faint, far wail" of the dead Milly becomes the substantive and displaced content of Densher's consciousness which along with the narrator's begins to dominate the latter part of the text. In this context it is worth noting the similarity of the narrator's and Densher's style to what Robin Lakoff describes as, the "polite" speech of American women which (as the bearer of social decorum) is prone to "hesitancy", "uncertainty", "hedges" and euphemisms, and to what she describes as the stereotype of women's discourse — "indirect, repetitious, meandering, unclear, exaggerated," making "wider use of the properties of implicature" (unlike male discourse which is "clear, direct, precise, and to the point").[24] The incorporation of femaleness, as historically recognizable and potent bearer of both subjectivity and social style, is the wider strategy of the text. Among other things, James is seeking to transfer and transform the intense personalism of the female mode *into* a transpersonal, transgender definition of the bourgeois consciousness — the absorption of femaleness is part and parcel of a larger social and ideological project.

The anxious proliferation of meaning is also tied to the renewed development of an aesthetic of hermeneutic freedom. This notion of 'freedom', itself honed on an epistemic split between instrumental necessity and non-instrumental aesthetic domain, partly produced in the Euro-American theatres of colonization, acquires a new significance at the turn of the century with the emerging contours of nationalist struggles in the imperialized formations and an intra-European struggle over them. As an American emigre, horrified at the possibility of the destruction of metropolitan 'culture', James' obsessive attempt to detach epistemological modes, by invisibilizing the worlds in which the enabling surplus is produced, appears in an ironic light. In wanting the reader to perform "quite half the labour[25]", the late Jamesian text is engaged in strenuous, extra-literary, salvage work. But on whose behalf ? In our context we may not only wish to reread our first relation to the late Jamesian text, but to recognise that its capacity simply to speak differently to different readers is perhaps less significant than the fact that it *still* encodes a culturally *usable* plurality, and still offers a model of literary "competence." It may well be the attraction of a privileged position in a hierarchy, the charm of inexhaustibility in a commodity culture, the lure of privacy, the guarantee of originality and the promise of self-governance which continue to encourage readers to write on James.

Notes

An earlier version of this essay entitled "The Desired and the Discerning critic of modernist Narrative: The example of Henry James" was published in *Journal of Literary Criticism*, vol4, no 2 (December 1987), pp. 32-46.

1. See for example Susan Kappeler, *Writing and Reading in Henry James* (London: Macmillan, 1980), pp. 52, 55.
2. See Kappeler, pp. 55, 74, 163, and Shoshana Felman, "Turning the Screw of Interpretation," *Yale French Studies*, 55/56 (1977), pp. 115, 155, 107, 166, 176.
3. Fredric Jameson, "The Realist Floor-Plan," in *On Signs,* ed., Marshall Blonsky (Baltimore: Johns Hopkins University Press, 1985), p. 382. Jameson points out that Flaubert's fiction, located in a transitional historical moment can offer different kinds of "interpretative *temptations*" which appear to "retain an objective existence" in the text.
4. Ralph Norrman, *The Insecure World of Henry James' Fiction: Intensity and Ambigu-*

not only, as Allon White notes, "the affinity between the enigmas of sexuality and the `play' of signification" which are a "a crucial generating complex of obscurity"[20] but also the "play" of money with the "play" of signification the consciousness undertakes. The analogy between money and consciousness, the identicality of their fluid operations becomes promiscuous at times; the play of money — "that perpetual passionate pecuniary purpose which plays with all forms, which derides and devours them"[21] — can expose the similarity of the superstructure of the consciousness with the base upon which and because of which it operates. Not only does each call into question the `value' of the other, they also threaten to become synonymous and so continuously devalue and destabilize each other. James is caught in the vibration of these, at bottom, social contradictions which are, however, conceived as enmeshed polarities — the prolonged moment of yearning and loathing, of revealing that he is concealing, encapsulates the discursive structure of his later work. Though the narrative secures and preserves the `modernist' notion of the `real' as residing in individual perception it is unable to deny or prevent the return of the determining `real'. Since rupture is always immanent in the way James conceives of these `opposing' forces, the defiantly infinite extension of "not knowing" becomes his line. Unwilling and unable to pay with the "lucid" he invests in a discourse of subtlety, hesitation, over-modification and uncertainty.

The Jamesian social relation is poised in the struggle to both acknowledge and transcend its materaility. There is both a desire to cash in on a particular historical moment in which the possibilities of 'freedom' for the materially well-endowed bourgeoisie seem vast as well as the recognition that these possibilities are gravely endangered, if not foreclosed, by the very materialism which enables them. Thus in the late Jamesian text there is a visible straining toward the sum possibilities of individual freedom and the startling though usually suppressed recognition of its conceptual and material limitations — both equally unavoidable for him in his chosen social location and in his historical moment. For James then the question is not one of choosing between alternatives but of making it impossible to choose between the antinomies which typify his fiction. The 'fatalism' of James' later work (encoded in the failure, entrapment, impotence or death of his protagonists) increases in the same proportion as does the narrative density and fecundity of the texts. The two are in fact identical, for if one side of the medal is failure the other side is success.

The radical transgression of form in its 'overdevelopment' (in its linguistic superfluity and in the structures of surrogacy) constitutes a major interrogation of nineteenth century juridical bourgeois morality and is at the same time a shift of bourgeois social morality into a new field of operation — the cognitive. Here morality is based on qualitative *acts* of cognition and representation (qualitative in this case *because* suffused with a special, exfoliating uncertainty) rather than on old-fashioned semantic content. The *act* of perception itself both becomes and betokens a kind of social style. Not only is understanding seen to reside in the act of perception (whether text's or reader's) but undecidability as a cognitive mode is infused with social value and social content. Premeditated difficulty becomes a mode of resisting certain forms of bourgeois complacency and consumerism as well as the site for forging and empowering a superior bourgeois consciousness. Further the uncertainty of the acts of cognition and representation and the accompanying secrecy and guesswork put a premium on the multiple interpretative possibilities of the text. The positive evaluation of uncertainty and difficulty privileges criticism and exegetical activity. Critical reading is situated as both a matter of minute textual exegesis and as a 'private' transaction between text and reader. The text itself makes a public value of the private life by articulating its cognitive structures and at the same time maintains its own (and the reader's) privacy by withholding or even refusing to publish the ground of such activity. The critic as constituted by the late Jamesian text is bound to be original: the contract the text enters into with its potential critic encodes the promise of ever subtler and more 'individual' reading — in other words the promise of renewability. Further the late Jamesian text presumes and creates a graded hierarchy of readers and critics which depends upon their *own* perception, sensitivity and responsiveness to the subjectivity of the characters and the complexity of the text as a whole.

James thus succeeds in canonizing an area of experience, in letting the margin flood the text in more than a literary sense. He legitimizes a particular style of bourgeois consciousness whose characteristics are an expansive sense of self, a tortuous relation to the social, a material density so palpable it nearly becomes a purer alternative to history, a sense of confidence and of fatality, a vision of possibility and a posture of passivity and renunciation. In fact the capacity of this consciousness to loop back on its own verities, to jeopardize the very act of perception it seeks to make primary, to be so knowing about "not knowing" makes of such a consciousness an infinitely plastic, agile, self-preserving mode whose self-doubt and self-irony serve to both pre-empt and subsume critique and so ensure its own resilience. The narrator's col-

6

Writing in Ourselves

Zakia Pathak*

As the title of this volume specifies, the period limit laid down by the editors is conceived in chronological terms. We might appear to transgress this boundary in choosing four works for scrutiny none of which were written in the nineteenth century. But then this essay is about ways of reading and it was in the late nineteenth century that those major interventions in thought — Marxism, psychoanalysis, anthropology, among others — were articulated and, as they developed, changed our perceptions of literary works and of the status of literature. Taken with later developments pertaining to critique, they made the project of this volume conceivable. If we begin by debating a central position of the editors (as expressed in the printout accompanying the invitation to contribute), we remain committed to their guiding principle that the study of English literature in the Indian university must always return us to what they call Ourstory.

I

It is disputable whether, as the editors of this volume believe, a work of English literature gives the Indian reader, by virtue of her positioning, signals other than it gives to readers in the producing culture. It is another and more urgent matter whether it should. Perhaps this issue is more profitably addressed by examining the nature of our commitment to teaching this literature at the historical moment that finds us engaged in doing so. On this commitment will depend the kind of criticism we bring to the work and the meanings we produce. For ourselves, teaching undergraduate students at a women's college at

---

* The grammatical marker of the first person throughout this essay, will take the plural form — we/our/us — since the essay represents a consensual position on pedagogical practice which emerged — and was constantly being refined — in continuing discussion with my colleagues, Saswati Sengupta and Sharmila Purkayastha. *Ave atque vale.*

Delhi University, we may state at the outset that our pedagogical practice is directed at producing from the literary "work" a "text" which engages with our concerns as Indians and women at the present time.[1] While respecting the cultural specificity of the work in the producing culture, we are committed to "making" a politics for it that will enable us to live our lives more critically.[2]

It is being increasingly recognised/resisted that the production of meaning is governed by ideological perspectives, implicit or theorised. "Even the most seemingly intuitive encounter with a literary text is ... already theory-laden ... there is no reading that does not bring to bear a certain context, interpret from a certain angle or set of interests, and thus throw one set of questions into relief while leaving others unasked."[3] We believe that our task as teachers is to create an awareness of these interests and thereby of the subject positions from which they emerge. The first objective of any political programme is to work towards an understanding that the contradictions of textual practice are the effect of a multiplicity of subject-positions, often perceived as contradictory and impossible to reconcile. Whether we then proceed to make it our responsibility to change the perceptions of interests by bringing to bear other contexts, other angles, is another issue, though in practice we have found that it is difficult to keep the two separate. "We need to see discourse structures in their fulness and power ... and the way to see one discourse is to see more than one."[4] We have had to be wary in classroom discussion of arousing resistances which might be counterproductive to our project, and so sometimes have to leave open the issue as to whether the subject position temporally privileged in the differential of identity is to be changed or cherished.

This exercise in cognition dramatizes more often than not, not the fractured subjectivity that might be expected given the disturbing impact of modernising trends upon traditional practices in the culture outside the classroom; but a unified, singularly untroubled subject. This subject is an effect of that "competence" which is acquired by a formal education in reading patterns, structures, codes.[5] Every literary work comes to us with encrustations from the metropolitan university and this form of intertextuality produces its own subject, also sometimes called the "informed" reader, who represents some kind of ideal. The literary perceptions of this reader when Indian connect only tangentially, if at all, with her understanding of the political and social problems she lives with outside the classroom. This separation between academic litspeak and the lay discourses of the culture,[6] between Academy and World, is tacitly permitted by a practice which histori-

ity (London and Basingstoke: Macmillan, 1982), p. 160. Norrman attributes this structure of chiastic inversion found in the language and characters of the late fiction to James' personal insecurity.

5. For detailed discussions see John Goode, "The pervasive mystery of style: *The Wings of the Dove*" in *The Air of Reality: New Essays on Henry James*, ed., John Goode (London: Methuen, 1972), and Elizabeth Allen's reading of the novel in her *A Woman's Place in the Novels of Henry James* (Basingstoke and London: Macmillan, 1984).

6. Henry James, *The Wings of the Dove*, New York Edition, vols. 19-20 (Fairfield: Augustus M. Kelley, 1976), 2: p. 341. Further references are cited in the text.

7. Ruth Bernard Yeazell shows how the language of the late novels does not allow the reader to "keep the minds of the narrator and his characters properly distinct" in her *Language and Knowledge in the Late Novels of Henry James* (Chicago and London: University of Chicago Press, 1976), p. 12; Leo Bersani demonstrates the difficulty of distinguishing precisely the characters expression of their thoughts from the narrator's presentation of them, or even from his comments, in "The Narrator as Center in *The Wings of the Dove*," *Modern Fiction Studies*, 6 (Summer 1960), p. 131.

8. Mark Seltzer says in somewhat different vein of *The Golden Bowl* that "the organic regulation of plot allows for a recession of narrative authority and makes for a dispersal of narrative control that is nonetheless immanent in every movement and gesture of character and plot." See *Henry James and the Art of Power* (Ithaca: Cornell University Press, 1984), pp. 87-88.

9. Terry Eagleton also points out that James does not "explode" the realist form to the extent of calling the "spectatorial ego into explicit question." See *Criticism and Ideology* (London: Verso, 1978), p. 145.

10. Margaret Walters, "Keeping the place tidy for the young female mind: *The Awkward Age*," in *The Air of Reality*, p. 202

11. J.P. Mowbray, "The Apotheosis of Henry James," *Critic*, 41 (November 1902), in *Henry James: The Critical Heritage*, ed., Roger Gard (London: Routledge and Kegan Paul; New York: Barnes and Noble, 1968), pp. 328, 331.

12. F.M. Colby, "In Darkest James," *Bookman* (America), 16 (November 1902), in *Henry James: The Critical Heritage*, p. 340; unsigned review, *Saturday*, 45 (January 1903), in Henry *James: The Critical Heritage*, pp. 332-33.

13. Tom Masson, "Mary's Little Lamb. In Different Keys," *Life* (4 May 1905), quoted in E.R. Hagemann "'Unexpected light in shady places': Henry James and *Life*, 1883-1916," *Western Humanities Review*, 24, no. 3 (Summer 1970), p. 247.

14. Vernon Lee, *The Handling of Words* (London: John Lane, 1923), p. 244, cited in Seymour Chatman, *The Later Style of Henry James* (Oxford: Blackwell, 1972), p. 58; Stephen Spender, *The Destructive Element* (London: Jonathan Cape, 1935), p. 197.

15. See for example William B. Stone "Idiolect and Ideology: Some Stylistic Aspects of Norris, James and Dubois," *Style*, 10, no. 4 (Fall 1976), p. 416-17.

16. Norrman, p. 180; Yeazell, pp. 35, 36, 130.

17. See Norrman on "verbalized unuttered utterance" in the late fiction, pp. 119-29.

18. Allon White says apropos the unopened letter that throughout the novel "James has signalled his rejection of that kind of narrative certainty, with its concomitant public affirmations — the novel begins to exclude the type of reader who expects and

demands these things in his reading: the refusal to open communication is fundamental to the narrative and authorial positions in it." See *The Uses of Obscurity: The Fiction of Early Modernism* (London, Boston and Henley: Routledge and Kegan Paul, 1981). p. 21.

19. Raymond Williams does not see James' fiction as solipsist, "since consciousness is social, its exploration, its rendering as a process, is connecting, inevitably." See *The English Novel from Dickens to Lawrence* (London: Chatto and Windus, 1970), p. 135.

20. White, p. 133.

21. Henry James, *The American Scene*, introd., Irving Howe (New York: Horizon Press, 1967), p. 111; see also Jean-Christophe Agnew's discussion of the way James' writing restructures feeling and perception "to accomodate the ubiquity and liquidity of the commodity form" in "The consuming Vision of Henry James," in *The Culture of Consumption: Critical Essays in American History, 1880-1980*, eds., Richard Wrightman Fox and T.J. Jackson Lears (New York: Pantheon, 1983), p. 68.

22. It is corporate too in the sense that it is "generated by the pervasive power of enormous corporation wealth;" see Eagleton, p. 142.

23. For a detailed discussion of James' incorporation of 'femaleness' see Kumkum Sangari "Of Ladies, Gentleman and 'The Short Cut'," *Feminist Readings of Literary Texts: Woman Image Text:* ed. Lola Chatterji (Delhi: Trianka, 1986).

24. Robin Lakoff, *Language and Woman's Place* (New York, Hagerstown, San Francisco, and London: Harper and Row, 1975), pp. 66, 73, 74, 73.

25. "Novels of George Eliot" in *Views and Reviews* ed. Le Roy Phillips (Boston: Ball, 1908), p. 18.

cizes the work in the producing culture but regards historical intervention in its reception as an inexcusable tampering with the truth of the work.

It is of course arguable that this separation between litspeak and culturespeak[7] marks the reception of a literary work in any culture, given the marginalisation of literature everywhere and that it is not peculiar to our situation as a once colonised people. However that may be, it is surely the case that where first-world texts are taught in a third world university the problem takes on a sharper edge. We seem to assent to the exertion of proprietorial rights of interpretation as expressed through the determination of interpretive paradigms by canonised criticism — which determine the production of meaning. Our pedagogical politics takes issue with such property rights. In a complex and ongoing process of abrogation and appropriation[8] we bring to the literary work other discursive paradigms which attract our own concerns.

This essay proposes to share our practice in teaching four texts prescribed in the undergraduate syllabus. In the section which follows, Section II, we read *The Book of Job* and *Murder in the Cathedral*. In our readings of both works we displace the paradigm of religion as revelation; it was the nineteenth century that subjected the Bible to Higher Criticism, eroding its revelatory status and opening up religion to other discourses. In *The Book of Job* we introduce the discourse of law which interrogates religious discourse. In *Murder in the Cathedral*, we identify an emerging discourse of nationalism and show how nationalist rhetoric was sought to be appropriated by church and state. These discursive paradigms enabled us to move into discussion of the major controversy of the present times, the Mandir-Masjid dispute. In Section III we are led from discourse structures to inscriptions. In two novels, Conrad's *Lord Jim* and Forster's *A Passage to India*, we show how the literary category of genre, far from being a neutral descriptive category, inscribes a reality. Ideological inscription is noted in the female psyche; and the political unconscious, it is suggested, may be gendered.

II

We began our engagement with *The Book of Job* by considering its status as a theodicy. First, we made the put-togetherness of its structure visible, by examining the process of inclusions and exclusions from the epics, folktales and poems of wisdom literature. By this means it could accommodate dissenting voices without compromising the theological centrality of Yahweh. Secondly, we showed how the Yahweh figure was an evolving creation of history, from the moody and capricious god who could only be propitiated to the Just god of the prophet Amos. Thirdly, we showed how religion constructed history, reading national disasters as visitations of God's wrath over infractions of Mosaic law. Later, individual histories problematised divine justice; when the law of retribution was extended to individual fates, undeserved suffering could not be explained. Fourthly, we brought in the discourse of law in the contemporary society by pointing to the Sanhedrin, which decided all cases of infraction of the law, including those arising from differing interpretations by the Scribes and Pharisees. Finally, quoting Hollander in Kermode,[9] we showed how religious texts are constituted by hermeneutical fiats; the Torah was strategically accommodated as the Old Testament while its historical dimension was disparaged and its truths projected as allegories, the true meaning of which could be found only in the Gospels. We concluded by suggesting that the agony of Job was that of a subjectivity fractured by contending discourses of revelation and law; identifying in the context the attendant machinery of proof, argument, intermediary and so on. Job's capitulation to Yahweh could be seen as a submission to the discourse of revelation dominant at that historical moment, against which the discourse of reason was still powerless.

This reading of *The Book of Job* enabled us to pass on to similar issues involved in the Mandir-Masjid Dispute — varying interpretations of religious texts, reluctance of the Hindu extremist organisations to subject the issue to a court of law, the debate among historians as to what were the facts of history, the possibility of a secular solution, etc. Just as the theological insistence on Yahweh as the one Supreme God was politically motivated to unite the people of Israel weaning them away from allegiance to previous Caanannite gods and so to consolidate them into a nation, so the primacy conferred on the Godhood of Ram was targetted, we suggested, to consolidating the Hindu vote in favour of a party which, projecting a Hindu nationalism, hoped to be catapulted into power.

We are aware that in making a politics for *The Book of Job* we are implicitly posing a form of historical essentialism between two countries divided by centuries of time and worlds of space. It may or may not be the case that we share similar histories; that is for the historians to debate. What is important is that we have arrived at this essentialism in positing a problematic in which empirical facts have played a part; and so hope to have avoided the odium attaching to that intuitive essentialism which is an a priori concept.[10]

It has been asked of us why in our reading of *The Book of Job* our feminist identity was not activated. Perhaps a recapitulation of the teaching process during the first term — August/September 1989 and January/February 1991 might go some way in answering that. We had at the start of the course suggested a few topics which might be discussed, among which was the marginal figure of Job's wife and her single utterance: "Curse God and die." Shortly afterwards, Mr. Advani's *rath* started rolling and tension escalated. Our reading the text as the conflict of two discourses, religious and legal, unequally empowered, was clearly an immediate response to the contemporary political scene. In other words, the feminist concern was temporally subordinated. It is not that different works foreground different subject positions; but that the subject position privileged in the differential of identity is responsive to the call for political action. If we were to teach the text today, the feminist perspective might well be privileged. We might then debate whether Sadhvi Ritambhara is articulating a new cultural code for women or exploiting a conservative one where a certain moral authority is accorded a public figure who renounces sexuality. Similarly, the large turn out of women in the B.J.P. rallies and marches which, they claim, marks a historical departure and a modernising trend, might be read as conservative, since it was in the cause of religion, as the women saw it. Certainly it was the conservative stereotype of woman, as the repository of sanity and compassion, that was encapsulated in the slogan of the Communist Party of India, during its women's rally at Ayodhya, which can be translated thus: "This is the cry of the Indian woman: Stop this slaughter!" The wife of Job was doomed to be silenced on both counts: she spoke against her God and against her husband.

Eliot's *Murder in the Cathedral* has traditionally called for a twofold approach. It is the story of a martyrdom and the baptism of people into faith by the blood of martyrs. It has also been tackled from the biographical angle where the author's eventual personal conversion to Catholicism is read as motivating the play. In our classroom practice these paradigms were displaced so as to recuperate a history read, under the Foucaultian paradigm, as the story of power which circulates in a network. The traditional concept of the freely-choosing individual, Thomas of Canterbury, rent by temptations but finally regaining that serene unity which he brings to his decision "out of time," to which his "whole being gives consent," was displaced by a multiply constituted subjectivity: the loyal subject of the King ("O Henry! O my King!") with whom he identifies ("I *was* the King, his arm, his better reason");

the servant of Christ ("No traitor to the king. I am a priest/ a christian, saved by the blood of Christ/ ... My death for his death"); the man of ambition ("The last temptation... to do the right deed for the wrong reason"). In this complex power struggle we isolated an emerging rhetoric of nationalism which imaged "England" on grounds of race, religion and class.

Tempter:	King is in France, squabbling in Anjou ...
	We are for England. We are in England.
	You and I my Lord, are Normans.
	England is a land for Norman
	Sovereignty. Let the Angevin
	Destroy himself, fighting in Anjou
	He does not understand us, the English barons.
	We are the people
Third Priest:	The Church is stronger for this action.
	Go, weak sad men ... homeless in earth or heaven
	Go where the sunset reddens the last grey rock of
	Of Brittany, or the Gates of Hercules
	Go venture shipwreck on the sullen coasts
	Where blackamoors make captive Christian men....
Tempter:	I am no trifler and no politician
	... I am no courtier ...
	It is we country lords who know the country
	And we who know what the country needs.
	It is our country. We care for the country.
	We are the backbone of the nation.

And against these definitions of the nation, there is that of the oppressed, the women of Canterbury, suffering because of the power struggle between church and state. They construct England in terms of the past conceived as golden:

A rain of blood has blinded my eyes. Where is England?
Where is Kent? Where is Canterbury?
O far far far in the past ...
It is not we alone, it is not the house, it is not the city that is defiled
But the world that is wholly foul

The "nation" is always constructed from the perspective of a set of interests. Moving to our contemporary political concerns, the foremost controversy today, tied up with the Mandir-Masjid dispute, which peaked during the general elections of 1989 and 1991 is the construction of Indian nationalism as Hindu. It was on the plank of Hindutva that the Bharatiya Janata Party won its spectacular electoral success in 1989 and was voted the largest opposition party in 1991. We discussed the attempt to appropriate nationalism with the class. It would however be illuminating if, carrying forward the paradigm of religion in conflict with other discourses, as in *The Book of Job*, we were to look at this problem in terms of the discourses of law and party politics. How does a party claim to represent the national interest and yet not attract the provisions of the Representation of People's Act (Section 123 (3) and 3(A)) of 1951? In a fascinating article in *The Times of India* of April 24, 1991, Rajdeep Sardesai lists the history of cases filed under this law. In a case before the Bombay High Court, the BJP/Shiv Sena lawyers, defending the "inflammatory" election speeches of Sena chief Bal Thackerey, claimed that the judges were using "western dictionary" definitions of Hinduism and were therefore unable to appreciate the contextual variance in a speech given in the local language and at a public meeting. It appeared to suffer transformation in the discursive situation of "the cold atmosphere" of the judicial chamber. In the Kunte vs. Prabhoo case of 1989, the BJP/SS alliance had insisted that Hindutva is a geo-cultural, even nationalistic notion. Justice Bharucha accepted that Hindutva had cultural connotations but ruled that the objective of Mr. Thackerey's speeches was patently and admittedly the protection of the Hindu religion. As for the slogan: "*Garv se kaho hum Hindu hain*" (Announce with pride that we are Hindus) — slogans were among the material facts filed — senior judicial functionaries felt that while in itself the slogan is unobjectionable under the law, if spoken at an election meeting it can be a corrupt practice inasmuch as a direct relation is being established between the candidate on the podium and the audience. Dr. Prabhoo was disqualified by the High Court. A woman lawyer and social activist, Vasudha Dhagamwar, entered the Hindu nationalism controversy from the columns of *The Indian Express* of 25 August 1989; arguing against the demand to abolish the canopy at India Gate since it is a memory of British colonial rule, she pointed out that nationalism by the time of the Second World War had gripped the *middle classes*. Leaders of the *lower caste* movement in the late nineteenth century, notably Jyotiba Phule, who had suffered at the hands of the Brahmins were on record as saying that they did not want the British to go. It is clear that statements derive their semantic value from the archive in which they are lodged. It is so with the term "nation". We can emerge from Eliot's play to a study of the dissemination of meaning in Indian political history.

III

With *Lord Jim*, we enter into the problematic area of the functioning of genre. Genres are not neutral descriptive categories; they institute a reality and inscribe a subject.[11] The Patusan story has been widely regarded in canonised criticism as a fantasy. But the fantastic is always inserted into a mimed reality against which it defines itself.

A genre may be defined as a mode and a structure.[12] Because fantasy is inserted into a mimed reality, the novel will contain the structural elements of both. The structural markers of realistic narrative are the focalisation of the hero, a scrutiny of the psychological motivation of his actions, disambiguation, i.e. effacement of all play with being/seeming and the effacement of utterance; this is the "text in a hurry."[13] The narrative is hitched to a mega-story which illumines it, creating expectations on the line of least resistance through a text already known. Historical and geographic names are stable semantic entities linking the text to the megatext, itself valorised. Against these criteria, Patusan defines itself as fantasy. Jim is focalised; the conflicting perspectives on his action so crucial a part of the Patna story are missing. There is hardly any psychological investigation of his actions ("It came to him ..."). There are no proper names which provide semantic stability. In one crucial respect, however, the narrative departs from the fantastic mode in that the utterance is almost effaced; the phatic and deictic signals so abundant in the Patna story are minimalised here so that Marlow's voice slides imperceptibly into something like omniscience. His framing of Patusan as a fantastic space has magnetised a whole line of critics — cloudcuckoo land, Edenesque, anti-paradise, a different time and space, something in a dream.[14] The competent Indian reader, reading off these signals, becomes complicit with the framing of the Orient and its representation as a land of intrigue and unrest, of lecherous rajahs and poisoned coffee, of talismanic rings which command fealty to the white man — finally, with the image of the white man bringing civilisation to a benighted people.

Now the canonised Todorovian theory requires that no poetic or allegorical reading be made since these destroy the fantasy (the moral of the animal fable is held to do this).[15] Also, that the hesitation of the reader suspended between two levels of interpretation, natural and supernatural, must be sustained to the end. It seems to us this condition coerces the reader into accepting the Orientalist reading of the Orient as a truthful rendering. It is our contention that this "hesitation" provides a space where a pedagogical politics can begin to operate. To choose to read referentially is to come across natural interpretations which might otherwise pass unnoticed in this dense text, as for instance the fact that Jim was the only man in Patusan who possessed gunpowder! To read referentially is to recuperate a recognisable reality where a land is violated by successive streams of invaders by armed might or by trade (the Celebes, the Europeans); where religion is exploited for power (Sherif Ali); where the invader initially colludes with a selected native power until he gradually gains supremacy (Jim with Doramin).

The realistic mode has fallen into some disrepute today because of its truth-claims. Notwithstanding, we suggest that so far as the white text is concerned the privileging of realistic markers yields a recognisable reality which puts us on guard against orientalist representations. Fantasy is today valorised because it is read as providing an alternative version of reality to which we can aspire and towards which we can work. This is a temporal (historical) construction of the genre which must be accepted if genres are to retain their explicative power. But spatial determinants must also be recognised in the construction of a genre; reading from here, Orientalist fantasy is not so much a subgenre of fantasy as a new function. Subversion and escapism do not exhaust the possibilities; fantasy can also operate to *subserve* a political reality.

As women, the figure of Jewel assumes a special importance for us. In most critical accounts, she is invisible; not surprisingly, since most critics leap from Stein to Gentleman Brown. In the shaping of Jewel, the structural markers of fantasy predominate. She has no proper name. She too is focalised; there are no disambiguating, psychologising perspectives on her actions. There is no play between being and seeming indeed Marlow's narrative iconizes her. She remains in the imagination in a series of fixed poses; always dressed in white, a high childish voice; an arm held aloft holding a torch; standing beside Jim's empty chair issuing commands of war; and finally, her black hair loose, her face stony, only the eyes straining after the shape of a man torn from her side by a dream. Her relations with Jim are romanticised: "They came together like knight and maiden, meeting to exchange vows among haunted ruins." Here Jewel is modelled after the Lady of chivalric romance, mystically conceived and sexually pure. But this figure too has to be inserted into the mimed reality. This exercise prompts the conclusion that the narrative attempts to mystify the realistic markers in order to emasculate their import in the white text.[16] Jewel's father and grandfather were white; among the possibilities which prevented her father from marrying her mother was "merciless convention." In all likelihood therefore Jewel is a half caste and illegitimate. In other words, she is located in the megatext in a history of miscegenation. Now, miscegenation always occurred outside matrimony. Whereas the thrust of this narrative is to present the relationship of Jim and Jewel as if within the matrimonial bond; "Jewel he called her as he might have said Jane, with a peaceful, marital homelike effect." "This was the theory of their marital evening walks." This repression of sexuality within the matrimonial bond constitutes Jewel as the Angel in the House; the iconicity of representation seeps into a stereotype of patriarchal discourse. Jewel is not the Kuchuk Hanem figure of Orientalist discourse, offering a more libertine, less guilt ridden sex, with the promise of untiring sexuality and of fecundity.[17] Patriarchal and Orientalist discourses are imbricated in the novel; the metaphor of the East as the bride ready to be unveiled by her lord is a recurring motif. Jewel's madness, in a referential reading, would qualify as that *anomie* which so often afflicted the English person in the colonies, cut off from his own kind.[18] Spilling over to the political story, it constitutes the Orient under white protection as fulfilled and flourishing.

As Schaeffer notes, the logic of inclusion has a radically ambiguous status since genres are temporally constructed. "Genre is always provisional because no immutable criterion decides whether any text belongs to a given genre ... This relation of inclusion calls for a decisional aspect irreducible to any definitional determinism."[19] By naming the genre to which Patusan belongs as Orientalist fantasy, we are led to perceive that Jewel is constituted at the intersection of generic traditions which repress female sexuality. This enables us to move towards considering the operation of the patriarchal stereotype in our own culture. It has been so deeply internalised as to be inscribed into the female psyche. Homi Bhabha defines the stereotype as a falsification not because it is a simplification but because it is "an arrested, fixated form of representation that in denying the play of difference constitutes a problem in the representation of the subject in social relations."[20] This stereotype is a site of combat in an ongoing debate of tradition versus modernity, where the Indian woman — *Bharatiya Nari* — is constructed as chaste and homeloving, god-fearing, living in and through her husband, even following him into the funeral pyre "voluntarily." In classroom discussion we have learnt not to simplify this ideology as male manipulation or female hypocrisy. There is an excess which cannot be contained in such formulations. At its worst it colludes with patriarchal power in an orgy of submission; at its best it sustains the institution of family, which we still valorise.

Our reading of Forster's *A Passage to India* (hereafter API) activated our racial and feminist identities. It would be more accurate to say that our critique of the generic operations of *API* was constructed by our subject position as Indian and a once colonised people. As such, we read the horror of miscegenation as inscribed in the political unconscious of the Englishman and as structuring the text. But in confronting

API with a recent novel by Deborah Moggach, *Hot Water Man*, (Jonathan Cape, 1982) which parodies it, our feminist identity provided a source for agency inasmuch as it enabled us to break out of the subject position which constructed the west as other. In the process it also raised the question as to whether the political unconscious is gendered.

The horror of miscegenation is vividly recounted by Ben Shepherd in his account of the case of Peter Lobengula, in the 1920s.[21] Lobengula was the son the African chief of Matabele, annexed by the British. He was brought to London as a part of a circus troupe, and met and married an English woman, Florence Jewell. The news threw Fleet Street into a frenzy. "Miscegenation has long been regarded as a crime against civilisation" *(The Spectator)*. "A stupendous act of folly and physical immorality" *(The Daily Mail)*. When approached to perform the marriage service, several members of the clergy refused. The general opinion was that "there is something disgusting in the mating of a white girl with a dusky savage." In India too the authorities were alarmed by signs of any intimacy between Englishwomen and Indian men. Lord Curzon refused permission to the Rajah of Puderkottai to proceed to England for the coronation since he suspected that he might marry an Englishwoman. It infuriated Curzon to see the daughter of the Duchess of Roxburgh dancing with the Raja of Kapurthala at Buckingham court.[22]

Early critical discussion placed Forster in the nineteenth century generic tradition of the bildungsroman. Even when his "mystical atheism" was appreciated, he was classed with the later Victorians like Butler and Meredith. Today in contrast, his work is perceived as belonging to a symbolist aesthetic; his use of symbol and a pervasive disquiet marks him as a modern.[23] It is in the Caves Section of the novel that the realistic mode is arrested and the social comedy turns sharply away from the direction it was headed for; even detective investigation is displaced by a metaphysical quest. We suggest that the horror of miscegenation was too deeply inscribed in the political unconscious to allow exploration in the realistic mode as was possible in Forster's Italian novel.

The manuscript drafts of the novel show that Forster was contemplating two possibilities in the Caves: a physical assault and a mutual embrace. It is conjectured that he abandoned this line of development out of weariness of marriage fiction and the man-woman relation. At the trial, not only does Adela withdraw everything because she cannot be sure of who followed her into the cave but the question itself suddenly loses interest for her, leaving Forster to pursue his metaphysical quest. "In fiction by woman," however, "the female domestic space of the romance is foregrounded as a form of value and power and self fulfilment."[24] Deborah Moggach's *Hot Water Man* suggests what could have happened in the caves "Through a double process of installation and ironising, parody signals how present representations come from past ones and what ideological consequences derive from both continuity and difference."[25] The blurb on the dust cover of *HWM* instals *API* unambiguously. *"Hot Water Man* must inevitably remind readers of *A Passage to India* as East and West meet once again in confusion." The encounter is updated. India is now post-independence Pakistan, the civil administrator is an executive in a multinational firm represented by the American Duke Hanson as well as the Englishman Donald Hanley. Donald and Christine are married and childless; the emotional relationship is also sterile. Like Adela, Christine is out to discover the real Pakistan, spurning the codes of the compound and haunting the bazaar. There she picks up a relationship with a Pakistani guide. This story climaxes with their visit to Gintho (which the narrator points out is an anagram for Nothing), noted for its cure of infertility. When Christine goes to the hot water springs, the guide stays behind in the guest house and goes to sleep. On her return she rapes him. "And how she had used him. She had confused and inflamed him ... she ... was the worst colonialist of them all." She becomes pregnant. The narrative — and the novel — ends on her relieved sobbing when the baby is delivered and she realises that the colour of its skin will not give her away. In the second narrative strand Donald, who is out to discover his grandfather's military past in all its splendour in India, discovers instead that he had a native mistress by whom he had had a child. Donald sets out to find his half-uncle and to make amends; but when he actually meets the man, he cannot connect. "Close up in the flesh it was impossible to believe that this man was his uncle. Perhaps he did not want to believe it. There was simply no connection" (p. 258). In the third narrative strand, Duke Hanson, whose wife is away in the States, has an affair with a Pakistani woman, educated at an elite school in England, professionally competent and with political connections useful to him. But he will not marry her. "You mean I've been your bit of fun on the side," she ripostes with bitterness when he gives her his feeble reason: "It just won't work." He swears that he meant it, to which she replies with dry anger: "You meant it with an eye on the fucking calendar." In an accusation reminiscent of Fielding's reprimand to Adela ("What have you been doing? Playing a game or studying life or what") she raves: "What on earth did you think you were doing? Having a little crosscultural communication? Getting to know the natives?"

IIWM is metafictional. It is process made visible by a mimesis of process.[26] In recuperating what might have happened in the Caves, it is ironic-parodic in naming the central silence of its progenitor. It exposes the duplicity which at least in part motivates the flight from realistic social comedy into a metaphysical dimension and a symbolist aesthetic: "the contradiction between ... the ideological project and the literary form which creates an absence at the centre of the text ... the text is divided, split."[27]

In a scandalous success of 1921, *The Sheik*, by E.M. Hull, the white heroine is raped by an Arab Sheik and after several repeat performances in the desert, learns to enjoy it. The concluding chapter discovers him to the heroine, and to the reader, to be the son of an English lord. *IIWM* spurns this duplicity. In moving interracial sex out of the genre of pornography and relocating it on the axis of race, *IIWM* exposes the limits of the liberal ideology which inspired *API*.

What is of crucial importance for the pedagogic enterprise is the meaning we produce from the conflictual relation between the two novels. From one perspective, *IIWM* is the discourse of Anglo-India for whom the metropolitan liberal Englishman was the other.[28] It is a fact of history that the Ilbert Bill, introduced in the nineteenth century to remove the provision that Englishmen in India could not be tried by an Indian judge, ran into violent opposition from the Anglo-Indian community and had to be withdrawn by the British government. From that perspective, *IIWM* in its derision of liberal self-delusion remains within the discourse of Orientalism, at its margins. We must decide if *we* wish to remain within the subject position which is an effect of that discourse. One way of breaking out — in the interests of a less factional perception which would be truer to our more complex relation with the west outside the classroom — which is invested with desire — is to locate *IIWM* in the counter discourse to Orientalism. Articulated by a female novelist, within the western culture, it suggests that the horror of miscegenation is inscribed in the white *male* psyche, and creates a gender affiliation across race.

IV

It will be evident by now that our pedagogical practice is heavily indebted to recent advances in critical theory that have opened up the concepts of author, text, reader and meaning. In acknowledging this debt, we lay ourselves open to the charge of being neo-colonialists; because in arguing for the validity of a response to English literature shaped by our perceptions of our contemporary political history, we ground these perceptions in European critical theory. This would qualify us as that "comprador intelligentsia" who "mediate trade in cultural commodities of world capitalism at the periphery."[29] By publishing abroad and in India we may be perceived as selling an India to the west and a west to India. Against this intelligentsia is posited the world of popular culture, unconcerned with problems of neocolonialism, borrowing freely from the west and refusing otherness: "anti national," asking only for "a simple respect for human suffering."[30] But it is the price we have to pay for engaging in the activity of critique that we should be crucially aware of our multiple subjectivity and how it is determined. We might regret but cannot regain that lost wholeness. Moreover, critique may also advance a claim to being anti-national inasmuch as it denotes "reflection on the conditions of possible knowledge and the system of constraints which are humanly produced."[31] As such it addresses a variety of structures of domination anywhere in the world. As third world readers of first world texts, our opportunities for intervention in political action are limited; it is in order to increase them that our pedagogical practice resists the hegemony of metropolitan critical traditions and contends for the kind of reception of texts we have described in this essay.

But opposition to these traditions is equally to be found within the metropolitan university. Is our debt to critical theory then a case of abrogation without appropriation? "The concern of the third world critic should properly be to understand the ideological sub-text which any critical theory reflects and embodies and the relation this sub-text bears to the production of meaning," says a black critic.[32] The ideological sub-text of critical theory, as we understand it, is oppositional thinking where structures of domination are perceived to be oppressive. We do not identify such thinking with a composite "Indian" response; we have positioned ourselves in this essay, as teachers at the university, as teachers of literature, as women, in fraught relation to other "Indians." To acknowledge this multiplicity of subject positions is not to valorise a fractured subjectivity as we have often been accused of doing. It is certainly to recognise our debt to critical theory, while still being moved by an imagined community of selves; and, going on from here, to try and forge a corporate identity for Miranda House; not by evading an identity crisis but by "staging" it.[33] This essay is another attempt towards that objective. And the history of such attempts could be the theme of another essay.

Notes

My thanks to Sharada Nair and Lola Chatterji for helpful comments. And to the Nehru Memorial Library for reading facilities.

1. Roland Barthes, *Image/Music/Text*, New York, Hill and Wang, 1977, pp. 155-64.
2. Tony Bennett, in A.P. Foulkes, *Literature and Propoganda*, London, Methuen, 1983, p. 19.
3. Gerald Graff, "The Future of Theory in the Teaching of Literature", *The Future of Theory*, Ralph Cohen, ed. New York, Routledge, 1989 p. 250.
4. Robert Scholes, *Textual Power*, Yale University Press, 1985, p. 144.
5. Jonathan Culler, "Literary Competence", *Reader Response Criticism*, Jane Tomkyns, ed. Baltimore, Johns Hopkins University Press, 1980, p. 116.
6. Gerald Graff, Ibid. pp 257, 269.
7. Here culturespeak is to be understood as lay discourse *about* culture.
8. "Abrogation is a refusal of the categories of the imperial culture, its aesthetic, its illusory standard of normative or 'correct' usage, its assumption of a traditional and fixed meaning inscribed in the words. It is a vital moment in the decolonising of the language and the writing of 'english', but without the process of appropriation the moment of abrogation may not extend beyond a reversal of the assumptions of privilege, the 'normal' and correct inscription, all of which can be simply taken over and maintained by the new usage", Bill Ashcroft et al, *The Empire Writes Back*, Routledge, London, 1989. p. 38.
9. Frank Kermode, *The Genesis of Secrecy*, Harvard University Press, 1979, p 18.
10. "... the recent revival of essentialism dating from the early 1970s ... stems from the ideas of Hilary Putnam and Saul Kripke and their insight that the knowledge of essences and of mary other necessary truths need not be *a priori*, need not, that is, be intuitively self-evident, and independent of all empirical confirmation or disconfirmation". Peter Crisp, "Essence, Realism and Literature", *English*, Spring, 1989. p. 55.
11. Christine Brooke-Rose, *"The Rhetoric of the Unreal"*, Cambridge University Press, 1981, p. 234.
12. Fredric Jameson. *The Political Unconscious*, London, Methuen, 1981 p. 107-10.
13. Phillippe Harmon, in Christine Brooke Rose, ibid, p. 85-94.
14. Frederick Karl, *Readers Guide to Joseph Conrad*, London, Thames and Hudson, 1960; C.B. Co, *The Modern Imagination*, London, Macmillan, 1986.
15. Christine Brooke-Rose, ibid, p. 68.
16. "Faced with the difficulty of telling Jim's story, Marlow does not arouse his audience's expectations; indeed he admits that love stories repeat themselves and are quite banal. Then he starts to talk, *somewhat mysteriously*, (italics mine), about a grave, the mother's grave, the mother's background, fate, the fate of distinguished women and eventually the grotesquely deformed tale of Jim's Jewel. Thus be man-

ages to add a touch of originality to a worn out archetypal topic". *York Notes*, Longmans, 1985, p. 37.

17. Edward Said, *Orientalism*, London, Routledge and Kegan Paul, 1978, pp. 6, 186-88, 190.

18. B.J. Moore-Gilbert, *Kipling and Orientalism*, London, Croom Helm, 1986, pp. 139-42.

19. Jean Marie Schaeffer, "Literary Genres and Textual Genericity", *The Future of Theory*, ibid, p. 177.

20. Homi Bhabha, "The other question: difference, discrimination, and the discourse of colonialism", *Literature, Politics and Theory*, Francis Barker et al, eds, London, Methuen, 1986, p. 162.

21. Ben Shepherd, "Showbiz Imperialism; the case of Peter Lobengula", *Imperialism and Popular Culture*, John Mackenzie ed. Manchester University Press, 1986 pp 94-112.

22. Kenneth Ballhatchet, *Race, Sex and Class under the Raj, 1793-1905*, Vikas, New Delhi, 1979, pp. 96-122.

23. Malcolm Bradbury; *Forster, A Collection of Critical Essays* (20th century views), New Delhi, Prentice Hall, 1979, pp 1-6.

24. Janet Batsleer et al, "Gender and Genre : women's stories," *Rewriting English : Cultural Politics of Gender and Class* (New Accents Series) Methuen, London and New York, 1985, p. 95.

25. Linda Hutcheon, *A Poetics of Postmodernism*, London, Routledge, 1989, p. 93.

26. Linda Hutcheon, *Narcissistic Narrative*, New York, Methuen, 1984. p 5.

27. Catherine Belsey, *Critical Practice*, London, Methuen, 1980. p. 107.

28. Brian Moore Gilbert, Ibid, pp. 7, 8.

29. Kwame Anthony Appiah, "Is the post in postmodern the post in post-colonial?" *Critical Inquiry*, Winter, 1991 Vol. 17. No 2 pp. 348.

30. Kwame Anthony Appiah, ibid, pp. 349-354.

31. Paul Connerton, ed. Introduction, *Critical Sociology*, Harmondsworth, Penguin, 1976. pp 17, 18.

32. Henry Lewis Gates, Jr. "Authority, (White) Power, and the Black Critic", *The Future of Theory*, ibid, p. 343.

33. Gerald Graff, ibid, p. 267.

7

Fiction or Historical Positioning ? :

A Reading of J.G. Farrell's
The Siege of Krishnapur

Sanjay Kumar

> History is a form of knowledge only through the relation it establishes between the lived experience of people of other times and today's historian.[1]
>
> Paul Ricoeur

*T*he Siege of Krishnapur is based on the happenings in Lucknow between May and November 1857. Farrell structures his work so closely around these happenings that he skirts the area between fictional and historical narrative. Writing in our time (the book was published in 1973), Farrell is aware of the problems that beset such an endeavour. His first task is one upon which many theorists have commented : the difficulties inherent in any attempt to combine history and fiction. Lukacs, who has written extensively on this area, asserts that fiction as a subjective creation can never make contact with or adequately represent objective reality which should be the point of focus in such a work.[2] The Italian theorist, Alessandro Manzoni, himself the writer of a historical novel, had focussed specifically on this problem much before Lukacs. To him, the attempt to combine history and fiction was open to two paradoxical kinds of criticism : "In certain historical novels . . . . fact is not clearly distinguished from invention and that, as a result, these works fail to achieve one of their principal purposes which is to give faithful representation to history" and on the other hand "in a given historical novel . . . the author does plainly distinguish factual truth from invention; this destroys the unity that is a vital condition of this or any other work of art."[3] Later writers, like Scholes and Kellog, have also felt that such an attempt must either produce a narrative which makes continual concessions to the empirical or totally abandon the empirical. This kind of text eventually becomes a form through which the artists try "to have their empirical bread and eat their fictional cake too."[4]

Apart from the juxtaposition of history and fiction, lies the problem of intentionality in the narrativisation of history. The "objectivity" of the historical fact and narrative has been challenged with increasing degree of success in the post-second world war years. This has, at times, led to assertions like Raymond Aron's "no such thing as *historical reality* exists readymade."[5] A historical narrative is also an aesthetic construct where the emplotment seeks to project the validity of the writer's conclusions. In the words of Hayden White : "Every historical narrative has as its latent or manifest purpose the desire to moralise the events of which it treats."[6] Given this "quasi-fictive character of the historical past"[7] (to borrow from Ricoeur), this paper seeks to determine the attitude of the artist/historian to his material to bring forth the moral centre of the book. The selection and organisation of historical material will be seen as intentional and contributive to the meaning of the text.

> Even if a relief now came, in many different ways it would be too late . . . and not only because so many of the garrison were already dead; India itself was now a different place; the fiction of happy natives being led forward along the road of civilisation could no longer be sustained.[8]
>
> The animal had managed to bite and tear itself free of its jacket but the sailor hat had defied all its efforts. Again and again, in a frenzy of irritation it had clutched at that hat on which was written *HMS John Company* . . . but it had remained in place. The string beneath its jaw was too strong.
>
> (193)

These two passages from *The Siege of Krishnapur* mark the parameters of Farrell's depiction of history. The first explicitly unveils the futility of the imperialist's endeavour. Taking a temporal position at the end of the 1857 uprising, the narrative voice appraises the act of colonising and condemns the concept of the white man's burden to be a fallacy. But the implications of the second reinforce the notions of British superiority that the first seemingly challenges. The intrinsically bestial, colonised nation can make a desperate attempt to rid itself of Britain (and thus of civilisation and culture, if we follow the logic of the torn jacket), but it cannot put a serious challenge to the might of the Englishman : "The string beneath its jaw was too strong." While in its explicit statements *The Siege of Krishnapur* seems to expose the sham ideals of imperialism, its implicit undertones, particularly in the treatment of history, reveal a pro-British imperialistic bias.

Farrell has received considerable praise from some western critics, including Margaret Drabble and John Spurling, for his treatment of history. Special mention has been made of his ability to both involve and disengage the reader as he proceeds "not just telling a story but history itself, from inside and outside"[9] This question of telling history from "inside and outside" brings us to the mode of historiography employed in *The Siege of Krishnapur*. Farrell's method of narrativising history provides a conglomeration of various contemporary schools. Unlike some historians who question the absolute character of an event, Farrell does not opt for a "dissolution of object."[10] The primary focus of the text is the upsurge of 1857 and within that, in particular, the events in Lucknow. But under this history of individual events he tries also to unfold "a history of gentle rhythms" with its "long-time span."[11] The attempt is to grasp deep under-lying trends, to delve into social history and bring forth what has been called the *mentalité* of the epoch. Studying attitudes regarding sex, love, death, ideology and religion, the historian of the *mentalité* tradition focuses on ethical values and behavorial patterns. Instead of merely telling the story of a dramatic episode he seeks to elucidate the internal workings of a past culture and society.[12]

At the very basic level Farrell seeks to make his observations on Krishnapur valid for the entire upsurge. At the outset there is a reference to the mysterious appearance of chapatis all over north India. Though the enigma has never been conclusively resolved, many historians have seen the chapatis as a signal for an uprising encompassing the whole of India. The book refers to the bursting of the upsurge in Meerut and its gradual spread all over north India with the native refusal to use the greased cartridges owing to a fear of a perversion of their religion. There is even an oblique reference to the economic exploitation of India as Mr. Simmons tells Miriam that each of the opium balls "would fetch about 75 shillings while to the ryot and his family the government paid a mere 4 shillings a pound" (89).

Taking a standpoint in the late twentieth century, the text goes to ostensibly provide a critique of Victorianism and imperialism. The narrative voice repeatedly focuses on the inner workings of the characters' minds to catch their thoughts which are often representatively Victorian. It is not only the magistrate's mind but also the Victorian's excessive trust in science which is the focus of the following passage : "The advance of science is not, the Magistrate knew, like a man crossing a river from one stepping stone to another. It is much more like someone trying to grope his way forward through a London fog" (115).

This exposé is enhanced by Farrell's ironic treatment of the British characters in the first half of the text. In the words of Frances B. Singh, he "uses the criticism of the English in India as a way of examining and passing judgement on some fundamental Victorian attitudes and beliefs."[13] The collector, besides his blind faith in science and progress, posits so much faith in discipline that he stifles his children in winter garments in the heat of Indian summer. The magistrate, the eternal scoffer, is laughed at for his obsession with phrenology and gets a deserved slap from Lucy for it. The padre too has an excessive faith in science and adheres to a scientific explication of religion. The two young heroes are fragmentations. Fleury, blessed with a poet's sensitivity, senses the gross materialism of the world around him and sees the limitations of scientific progress. But he is too much the poet and introduced with his obesity and the nickname `Dobbin' (which riles him) he remains incongruous as the hero of a mutiny novel. Harry, on the other hand, is too much the man of action. His logical faculties have developed at the cost of his affective sensibilities. The two together are stereotypically ridiculous. They get embarrassed before dirty pictures, look down upon a woman who has experienced premarital sex and are surprised that a woman has pubic hair. The ridicule extends to the memsahibs too. If before the uprising they are as unaware of the developments around them as Mrs Dunstaple, once the siege begins their vanity stands conspicuous. They assert their class-consciousness even in the face of death and nowhere are their pretensions more apparent than in the treatment accorded to the "disgraced" Lucy. Hers is "the only bed that had any space around it, for even Louise's bed, which was next to hers, stood at a small but eloquent distance" (173). The characters become more ridiculous in their interactions. This can be seen in the padre's attempt to convert Fleury from his emotional faith into a rational acceptance of the existence of God in the teeth of enemy bullets. It is more obvious in the tussle between the two padres over burial space even before anybody from either sect has expired.

The text reveals the chasm that separates the British culture from the Indian. This divide ensures that the British will remain a superimposition on India and all apparent acceptance of British ways by the native is merely on the surface. Fleury, for example, is confronted with a "contradiction" soon after his arrival in India : "wealthy Indian gentlemen also gave balls in Calcutta in the civilised European manner, even though at the same time they despised English ladies for dancing with men as if they were 'nautch girls' " (42). The gap is again evident in the treatment given to British attempts at charity by the native Christians : the sugarfruit is thrown away because "although Christians, many of them considered themselves Hindus as well, indeed primarily, and had no intention of being defiled like the sepoys with their greased cartridges" (131). Farrell uses the perspective of chronological time to further demonstrate the futility of the British endeavour. This is manifest, above all, in the change wrought in the collector. The man wonders at the beginning of the siege: "Why after a hundred years of beneficial rule in Bengal, the natives should have taken it into their heads to return to the anarchy of their ancestors" (176). He reaches a more pessimistic conclusion during the siege : "Would science and Political Economy ever be powerful enough to give them a life of ease and respectability ? He no longer believed that they would" (223). In the last chapter, deliberately placed in 1880, more than two decades after the restoration of British hegemony, the collector is convinced that "culture" is a "sham" : "a cosmetic painted on life by rich people to conceal its ugliness" (344). And with this realisation are abandoned his efforts at "reforming" human beings together with his faith in science and progress. These assertions together with the oftcited last sentence of the book : "Perhaps, by the very end of his life, in 1880, he had come to believe that a people, a nation, does not create itself according to its own best ideas, but is shaped by other forces of which it has little knowledge" (345), could lead us to a conclusion that the text transcends social history too for a foray into what Braudel calls the realm "that is almost changeless, the history of man in relation to his surroundings."[14] We could endorse the view that the text not only debunks imperialism but is a detached narrative which involves larger themes like "history's malevolence towards human beings"[15] or "seeks to define the meaning of historical consciousness and show how it is developed."[16]

However, the history of events with its "short, sharp and nervous vibrations"[17] militates against such a view. Farrell's biases emerge in his selection and interpretation of events together with the depiction of Indians in the uprising. In the 1857 upsurge, Farrell has chosen an extremely controversial occurrence. The mindless cruelties indulged in by both sides made it practically impossible for Englishmen and Indians of the nineteenth century to talk about the upsurge without emotional prejudice. For the English, the upsurge is linked with notions of the Raj. They see it merely as a sepoy mutiny and its suppression as an assertion of British arms and generalship. The Indians, on the other hand, have stressed its popular aspect and seen in it the first manifestation of "national" feeling.[18] In the Afterword to the text Farrell stresses that besides available official records he has used the journals of two people who participated in the siege - Maria Germon, the wife of an officer and H.S. Polehampton, the priest of the garrison. While choosing from the accounts available, Farrell omits those that even marginally challenge the superiority of the British. The imperialistic bias of the text emerges on its comparison with the correspondence between British officials of the period.

After the initial rebellion at Alambagh and Lucknow, the British forces fought against the rebels at Chinhat on the 30th of June. The battle proved to be Lawrence's pitfall. All accounts of it in diverse letters of the time testify the ineptitude of the British forces and the courage and generalship of the rebels. The letter written on the 26th of September by Brig. J.E.M. Inglis to the Secretary to the government states :

> The force, exposed to a vastly superior fire of artillery and completely outflanked on both sides by an overpowering body of Infantry and Cavalry, which actually got into our rear, was compelled to retire with the loss of 3 pieces of artillery, which fell into the hands of the enemy. . . . and with a very grievous list of killed and wounded.[19]

Maria Germon, whose journal Farrell has, in his own words, "cannibalised," says of Chinhat in the entry of June 30th:

> It had proved far different to the glorious expectations that had been excited on first starting, for the Native Artillery proved faithless and the enemy being in far greater numbers than the spies had led us to believe, our little party was surrounded and it was only a wonder any escaped to tell the tale. . . . It was a fearful morning never to be forgotten.[20]

But Farrell forgets that morning. There is no reference to the battle of Chinhat, disastrous for the British and glorious for the rebels, in *The Siege of Krishnapur*.

Following the defeat at Chinhat was the death of the redoubtable Henry Lawrence, recorded in every letter and official statement. The letter cited earlier states : "on the very next day (2nd July) he was mortally wounded by the fragment of another shell which burst in the same room, exactly at the same spot."[21] A day before a shell had burst in the same room and officers had asked Lawrence to change his room but Lawrence had characteristically scoffed the fear of his subordinates. The second had burst on the 2nd of July and resulted in his death. Thereafter Inglis took command of the garrison. In *The Siege of Krishnapur* the collector survives the siege. There is a death early in the book but of general Jackson (there was a Coverly Jackson who had the charge of Lucknow before Lawrence took over) whose senility is all too evident and he is never the focus of our attention. The defence of Krishnapur, from the beginning to the end, is in the hands of Mr. Hopkins. Like Lawrence, the collector also faces two shots. The first time "he instantly dropped to the floor in fear" (159), but he has become a braver man the second time and remains seated while the subalterns with whom he is having tea instantly jump under the table. He has impressed them, and hopefully us, with his "sangfroid" (201). He falls ill and suffers from excruciating pain from erysipelas. But his superior character is evident as he rallies to overcome not only personal illness but deaths of colleagues and other hardships to raise the morale of the garrison. A representative case is his exhortation to the people of the garrison, as they auction the food supplies of their dead comrades, not to surrender to despair and "profit from each other's misery" but "all starve together and all survive together" (259). Farrell deliberately omits the defeat of British forces and the death of their commander because he intends to project them as invincible. Further evidence of this is in the battle scenes.

The disengagement that the author has been trying to maintain in the first half of the narrative gradually disappears once the defence of the residency begins and the text gets heavily skewed to extol the British. Contrasted against the rallying together of the British community is the behaviour of the natives. They "in a cheerful and multifarious crowd assembled everyday beneath awnings, tents and umbrellas to watch the *feringhees* fighting for their lives" (194). The Englishmen, surprisingly inclusive of the sensitive poet Fleury, show their worth as soldiers. First, Cutter successfully springs a mine under the rebels. Then, despite depleted forces, the British garrison repulses the successive attacks of the natives. And finally, as the British slaughter hundreds of native soldiers and escape into the trench, Harry, with just the right amount of elevation and proper loading explodes the sepoy magazine :

> When at last he was satisfied with the elevation he supervised the loading; a dry wad over the cartridge and then a damp one : Then he ordered Ram to serve out the reddest shot he could find in the furnace, watched it loaded and motioning the pensioners back, himself touched it to the vent. There was a crash. The cannon did not burst. A small glowing disc swam calmly through the clear morning . . . . It dipped swiftly then towards the magazine and smashed through the flimsy, improvised roof.

(329)

This is British accuracy in the handling of ammunition and in the framework of the text, beyond the reach of native comprehension.

The passage quoted above invites comparison with numerous jingoistic passages in early mutiny novels designed to show British supremacy on the warfront. To cite an example from Flora Annie Steel's *On the Face of the Waters* (1896) :

> A little puff of white smoke went skywards first, and then slowly, majestically a great cloud of rose-red dust grew above the ruins, ... It hung there for hours. To those who know the story it seems to hang there still, - a bloody pall for the many, for the Nine, a crown indeed.[22]

The comparison begs the question of the relation between today's western artist/historian and the lived experience of people in the colonised world. Has he, despite pluralism and dialogic positioning, moved beyond showing down the "Pandy" and evidencing racial superiority ?

The most glaring example of distortion of source material in *The Siege of Krishnapur* is regarding the relief of the Residency itself. Besieged after the battle of Chinhat on the 30th of June, the garrison was finally relieved on the 14th of November. The epic siege really consisted of two consecutive sieges. Havelock and James Outram reached Lucknow with their forces after the middle of September. The journey was by no means easy. The rebels fought bravely and desperately before yielding ground as the letters of the two generals testify. In a letter written to the commander-in-chief on the 6th of August Havelock concedes : "The enemy is in such force at Lucknow that to encounter him five marches from their position would be to court annihilation."[23] Outram corobborates the strength of the rebels : "The resistance was more obstinate in the suburbs, and at a great sacrifice the troops forced their way to the garrison at Lucknow."[24]

The first relief was little more than a reinforcement. Successful in forging their way in, the combined forces of Havelock and Outram could not force their way out. Maria Germon's journal testifies the futility of the first relief : "They took nine guns and did their work well, although we can scarcely call this a relief seeing we have to feed the new troops on our own scant rations and have them in consequence further reduced."[25] Relief was finally brought by the forces of Sir Colin Campbell on the 12th of November, nearly two months later. The rebels again fought tooth and nail as the British forces slowly defeated them at Dilkusha Park, Shah Najaf, Moti Mahal and Secunderbagh. Again the fighting was particularly grim in the streets, lanes and compounds as Sir Colin Campbell's letter to the Governor General written on the 18th November testifies:

> This place (Secunderbagh) is a high-walled enclosure of strong masonry, of 120 yards square, and was carefully loopholed all round. It was held very

strongly by the enemy. Opposite to it was a village at a distance of a hundred yards, which was also loopholed and filled with men.... This position (Shah Najaf) was defended with great resolution against a heavy cannonade of three hours.[26]

Victory would not have been possible if the Lucknow garrison had not taken an active part creating diversions and finally blowing intervening walls and houses to join Campbell's forces at Secunderbagh.

In *The Siege of Krishnapur* the two hard-fought reliefs are contorted into one easy victory. British supremacy is asserted with a singular, decisive and irrevocable stroke. There is no resistance and the rebels flee from around the Residency hearing the arrival of the British forces. It is true that the might of the British forces did succeed in ultimately suppressing the rebels but Farrell presents heroism and courage as exclusive British traits.

The only detailed study of an Indian in *The Siege of Krishnapur* is that of Prince Hari and the portrait is far less flattering than those of the British. So enamoured is he of scientific "forwardness," which some British characters (like Fleury) see as suspect, that Hari tries blindly and moreover, incapably to ape the British. "A boiled egg and Blackwood's is the best way to begin" (80) his day. Hari proudly displays his possessions, western and eastern examples of "science and progress" before Fleury. While asserting their worthlessness, he obviously expects Fleury to contradict and congratulate him. The images of his father that remain in our minds are of a man "breaking wind" while "asleeping" (84) and of being charged at by a buffalo. The British characters too become butts of ridicule, but using a relative yardstick Farrell places them on a pedestal vis-a-vis their Indian counterparts. This becomes all too obvious in the final section as the English grow through their participation in the siege. Fleury develops to combine action with his thinking faculties. Apart from the collector, the padré too realises the foolishness of his faith in science and progress and sees the Great Exhibition as "the World's Vanity Fair." Above all, Louise transforms from a "pale anaemic-looking girl, who had once thought only of turning the heads of young officers" to "a young woman of inflexible will power" (332). Contrasted to them is the last view of Hari:

> Around him lay scattered the festering remains of half a dozen meals. There was a powerful stench of urine also, as if he no longer went outside to perform his natural functions. He had turned grey, *as Indians do when they are unhappy* (Italics mine).

(231)

The point of this comparison is not to say that people like Hari and his father were not there in India at that time, but that they are the only members of the Indian community that Farrell posits and further, he shows development and growth to be possible only in the British character. If we agree with Curtin's formulation of the "key beliefs" of western imperialism — "(a) Non-western culture is far inferior to that of the west. (b) Non-western people are racially different from Europeans, and this difference is hereditary. (c) Therefore, the cultural inferiority is also hereditary."[27] — then is not *The Siege of Krishnapur* an imperialistic text?

The sepoys who actually rose against the British are non-existent for the writer except as a disorganised rabble who, despite a massive superiority in numbers and ammunition, could not make much of an impression on the garrison. The sepoys shown individually are pathetic examples. The first sepoy that Fleury encounters is seated upon a horse and has a drawn sabre in his hand, but the unarmed Fleury manages not only to unharness him but also to break his collar-bone in the bargain. The second has Fleury at his mercy but cannot execute because he is calmly shot down by Harry. A third is ridiculously dancing around Chloe, with a drawn sabre, within enemy lines and is shot dead by Ram. Another is a giant-sized sepoy who grapples with a much smaller Fleury towards the end of the book. Despite being close to death, David finally blows Goliath to smithereens with a multi-barreled pistol because David is British and heroism and good fortune are British prerogatives.

In Awadh, in particular, the rebellion was popular and the rebels were well-organised. The popular basis of the revolt has been asserted by many British historians. R. Hilton in *The Indian Mutiny: A Centenary History*, while asserting that the mutiny was not "at all a popular uprising against an oppressive or reactionary British tyrrany," concedes that "Oudh was, in fact, the only part of India where the great rising of 1857 assumed anything like the appearance of a national movement against the British."[28] The revolt had a popular base because of the involvement of the talukdars, the petty landowners who had been dispossessed as a result of the economic policies of the British. Three talukdars, Beni Madho, Man Singh and Madho Singh, deserve special mention. After the battle of Chinhat they forged an alternate government, played a pioneering role during the siege and even after the relief continued fighting in the rural countryside.[29] Repeated references to them are found in the letters of various officers. A letter written by the Governor General as early as the 27th of April shows that the British too felt that the talukdars had been harshly dealt with: "I was not surprised to see in your letter that some of the talookdars have been hardly dealt with (sic) — many — if Mr. Jackson's account was correct."[30] To Man Singh alone there are at least three references and the letter of Governor General dated 12th September shows that the British were constantly trying to wean away the talukdars with diverse offers of compromise and agreements:

> Maun Singh may be assured that if he continues to give the Governor General effective proof of his fidelity and goodwill, his position in Oudh will be at least as good as it was before the British government assumed the administration of the country ... The same assurance may be given to any other chiefs, who will be rewarded in proportion to the support which they may afford.[31]

In *The Siege of Krishnapur* there is not even a passing mention of the bravery of the sepoys, no reference to the talukdars or to the popular or even the military composition of the rebel forces. Farrell interprets the word "siege" in its passive and secondary connotation as the period of besiegement and ignores totally the positive connotation of the operations of the attacking force. The focus of the text remains unerringly the defence of the British garrison. It highlights their oddities, their squabbles, their fortitude and above all, their heroism. And the moral drawn from Farrell's organisation of his material is not significantly different from that drawn by Sir William Kaye from the upsurge in his famous three volume *History of the Sepoy War* (1867), published more than a century before *The Siege of Krishnapur:*

> The story of the Indian Rebellion of 1857 is, perhaps, the most signal illustration of our great national character ever yet recorded in the annals of our country. It was the vehement self-assertion of the Englishman that produced this conflagaration; it was the same vehement self-assertion that enabled him, by God's blessing to trample it out.[32]

Like Kaye, Farrell too succumbs to racial prejudice. But unlike Kaye's work, Farrell's *The Siege of Krishnapur* is insidiously partisan. It positions itself in our time, purports to be a debunking of imperialism and ends up presenting yet another saga of the heroism of the white man.

Notes

1. Paul Ricoeur, *Time and Narrative,* trans Kathleen McLaughlin and David Pellaver (Chicago and London: U of Chicago P, 1984) 1: 99.
2. The questions are raised particularly in two of Lukacs' works: *The Theory of the Novel* and *The Historical Novel.*
3. Alessandro Manzoni, *On the Historical Novel,* trans. Sandra Bermann (London: U of

Nebraska P, 1984) 63, 65.
4. Robert Scholes and Robert Kellog, *The Nature of Narrative* (Oxford: Oxford UP, 1966) 246.
5. Raymond Aron, *Introduction to the Philosophy of History: An Essay on the Limits of Historical Objectivity*, trans. George J. Irwin (1938; Boston: Beacon P, 1961) 118.
6. Hayden White, "The Value of Narrative in the Representation of Reality," in *On Narrative*, ed. W.J.T. Mitchell (1980; Chicago and London: Chicago UP, 1981) 14.
7. Ricoeur, *Time and Narrative*, 3: 191.
8. J.G. Farrell, *The Siege of Krishnapur* (1973; Harmondsworth: Penguin, 1979) 249. All further references are to this edition and page numbers follow the quoted passage in the text.
9. John Spurling, "As Does the Bishop," in *The Hill Station*, ed J.G. Farrell (Harmondsworth: Penguin, 1981) 147. Margaret Drabble's "Things Fall Apart" is also in the same edition.
10. Aron, 118.
11. Fernand Braudel, *On History*, trans. Sarah Matthews (Chicago: U of Chicago P, 1980) 3, 25.
12. Georges Duby, *The Three Orders: Feudal Society Imagined* trans. Arthur Goldhammer (Chicago and London: The U of Chicago P, 1980), provides a good illustration of the *mentalité* tradition.
13. Frances B. Singh, "Progress and History in J.G. Farrell's *The Siege of Krishnapur*," in *Colonial Consciousness in Commonwealth Literature*, ed. G.S. Amar and S.K. Desai (Bombay: Somaya Publications, 1984) 200.
14. Braudel, 3.
15. Spurling, "As Does the Bishop," 159.
16. Singh, 200.
17. Ricoeur, 1: 103
18. There are hardly any records of the sepoys' side of the story because they worked clandestinely and were finally crushed. For the "facts" of the mutiny, a historian has to rely almost exclusively on British correspondence and official rewards. All contemporary English accounts show their anger and thirst for revenge and their accuracy is questionable. Even the thoroughly researched early "histories" of Sir W. Kaye, Charles Ball and G.W. Forrest are marred by an anti-Indian bias. Indian accounts, the first being V.D. Savarkar's, also manifest a jingoistic prejudice.
19. G.W. Forrest, ed., *Selections from the Letters Presented in Lucknow and Cawnpore, 1857-58* (Calcutta: Military Department P, 1902) 38.
20. Maria Germon, *Journal of the Siege of Lucknow* (London: Constable, n.d.) 53.
21. Forrest, 39.
22. Flora Annie Steel, *On the Face of the Waters* (1896); Delhi: Arnold-Hienemann, 1985) 157.
23. Forrest, 172.
24. Forrest, 228.
25. Germon, *Journal*, 100.

26. Forrest, 340, 342.
27. Philip D. Curtin, *Imperialism* (London and Basingstoke: Macmillan, 1971) xvii.
28. Richard Hilton, *the Indian Mutiny: A Centenary History* (London: Hollis and Carter, 1957) 18, 17.
29. In what was an Oxford thesis, later published as a book, *Awadh in Revolt* (Delhi: Oxford UP, 1984), Rudrangshu Mukherjee stresses the organisation and popular base of the rebels. The fourth chapter deals specifically with the siege of Lucknow and the spread of the revolt to the countryside by the talukdars. After Chinhat, Jalail Singh was the chief spokesman, Birjis Qadr the crowned king and as he was a minor the reigns were in the hands of Hazrat Mahal. The rebels also had a parliament which was under the control of the soldiers. Above all, more than sixty per cent of the fighting force at the siege of Lucknow was drawn from the general rural populace.
30. Forrest, 3.
31. Forrest, 36.
32. J.W. Kaye, *History of the Sepoy War* (1967; London: Hale, 1880) 1: xiv.

8

Of Indian History and English Studies: A Discussion

[*This discussion is based on an interview the Ourstory editors had with Prof. Bipan Chandra. A few questions were read out to him in the beginning as much to make clear the framework of the discussion as to give him an occasion initially to formulate a general statement. Once it had been made, other pointed questions, queries, comments, agreements-disagreements followed. In spite of his characteristic sweep, Chandra remained precise in his responses and illustrations, thus providing a sharp focus to the issues connected with the inter-working of history and literature. The purpose of the interview was not to arrive at a mutually agreed position at the end but to have a meaningful and open-ended dialogue. As a matter of policy, the editors intervened only when it was necessary, allowing the interviewee to speak most and sort out matters on his own. Interventions of the editors from the first cluster of questions onwards have been given in italics. The text in the regular type belongs to Chandra.*]

Questions

1) *What is the significance of the tremendous attention that has been focussed on nationalism and colonialism by Indian historians? Does it have a direct bearing on the political situation today?*

2) *Pan-nationalism has come for severe questioning on grounds of religion, race, language, etc. Is it just a coincidence that centres of these agitations have been in the northern part of the country — whether Naga, Bodo, Jharkhand, Gurkha, Punjab, Kashmir, Ram Janambhoomi?*

3) *In case one agreed to the premise that these agitations have their centre in the North, is there a relation between this development and the form Nationalism took in the 19th century?*

4) *In the analysis of historical developments in India, are the Indian subaltern historians putting forth a theory of history which is in-*

digenous?

5) *What is the extent of indebtedness of our historians to "western" theories?*

6) *A related question: with the emergence of a changing perspective of Nationalism, has there actually been a corresponding shift in the understanding of historiography, especially in the light of theories emerging in the west which see historical fact as a construct determined by shifting historical forces?*

The session will naturally lead to cutting across the various questions, but it would be a good idea if we went by a distinct question plan. This will provide a focus.

Good you have framed it like this. Let me make the point clear at the very beginning. The word "Nationalism" as we use it in India is different from the way the word has come to be used in Europe in the 18th and 19th centuries. English being the language of our political and intellectual expression, we borrowed and used this word. Also, our anti-imperialist struggle started in the 19th century when nationalism was just coming into its own in Europe. And in Europe there was the German struggle for unification, the Italian struggle for unification and expulsion of foreign influences, the Greek war of independence, the Romanian struggle for independence, the Polish struggle for independence from Great Britain. We also borrowed this word from there in that context. In the 20th century, on the other hand, national movements, or national liberation movements are anti-imperialist movements. They were started in other countries of Asia and Africa much later than ours. The Chinese adopted an anti-imperialist position only after the First World War. Before that they were not able to distinguish between anti-Manchu and anti-foreign positions. In fact, their tallest leader even expected that foreign banks and foreign capital will develop in China. He wrote a book in 1916 to that effect. Similarly, the Egyptian struggle for freedom began properly after 1918. The Vietnamese kept on struggling against the French from the day of conquest as did the Africans but their movement was a traditional struggle in the same way in which our resistance was traditional in 1770, 1810 — ending with the revolt of 1857. In Vietnam, the proper anti-imperialist struggle began in the 1920s as also in Africa in the 30s, 40s and 50s. Consequently, most of them were not dominated by England. Therefore, they started using another term under the Communist influence as many of these movements were led by Communist parties. They used the term "national liberation movement" or "national liberation struggle." Now what we call national movement is the same as what they call national liberation struggle. But a lot of confusion is there, specially in India, and specially among Indian Marxists and very much among subalterns who don't make the distinction. They think national movement is different from nationalism, but nationalism in India is the same as national liberation in other parts of the world. Its nomenclature is national movement because our movement came in the 19th century, while these came later after the First World War. A very simple question to consider is: Is the National Movement in India a subaltern movement or an elite movement? — a basic question subalternists have raised. In the fifties the question was different. There was an American historian/political scientist Johnson who raised the question regarding China. The question was raised in India. Was Indian nationalism peasant or bourgeois or working class? Very interestingly, this question is never asked regarding Vietnam. I would say China, too, but Vietnam is a better example. Now, was the Vietnamese movement bourgeois? Was it peasant nationalism? Rubbish. No Vietnamese would agree that the movement there was peasant-nationalism. Was Chinese National Movement Communist-led or anti-imperialist? The Chinese Communist historians attacked it frontally. Was Vietnamese liberation movement a working class liberation movement? Of course not. Was it bourgeois? That would horrify any Vietnamese. So what was the Vietnamese movement led by Ho Chi Minh? Similarly, the Chinese movement: Is it a working class national liberation movement? No. Is it peasant national liberation movement? No. Is it bourgeois national liberation movement? No. Then what was it? This question is raised regarding India only because the term national liberation movement is not used here.

But in India, isn't it also the question of the formation of a nation state?

That is a different question. But first you asked about nationalism. Nationalism in Europe was born as a result of the effort to free their societies from feudal domination. At that time the working people were not a major component of the struggle. It was between the bourgeoisie and the feudal class. For the first time in the French Revolution the reassessment came in a big way. It did not come in the English revolution of 1640 and anyway English historians would no longer call the 1640 revolution a bourgeois movement. Therefore, in Europe nationalism was first born as an effort of the bourgeoisie to free itself and the economy from feudal domination. However, in the second half of the 19th century, with the advanced capitalist countries becoming imperialist, i.e. they colonised and exploited other societies, nationalism became a movement to keep their own working people satisfied with their lot by glorifying imperialism. So nationalism was what we call chauvinism. Nationalism as an ideology in Britain was the ideology of "the sun never sets on the British empire." It was the ideology of Rudyard Kipling, of Disraeli, Gladstone and others. Similarly, in Germany "we want our place in the sun;" in France, it was the "civilising mission." Nationalism, thus became the ideology of the ruling classes in order to continue their domination over people in an age of democracy. This ideology took a very aggressive and developed form (this is true of literature also). Even Marx believed in 1850s that whenever adult franchise comes, the liberation of working people will come. It was assumed that if everybody can vote, the poor being 95% are bound to have their own government. What was not realised was that the poor would be persuaded through ideological instruments, what Gramsci calls "ideological hegemony," to vote for the same old parties even though democracy had come. So in Britain when the final reform act came and there was adult franchise, it was not even Gladstone but Disraeli, the conservative, who won the elections of 1877. There nationalism was first a bourgeois movement against feudalism, but later it became a bourgeois movement against their own working people.

We were dominated by colonialism, i.e. by foreign economic and political structures, whether directly as in India or indirectly as in China. Therefore, in our countries the struggle was of all the exploited people. It was not only the bourgeoisie that was interested in abolishing feudalism but the entire society. One has to realise that our movement which started in 1880s is very much the same as the movement in China or Cuba or Egypt or West Asia. Which ideological trend, which party, which leadership is at the head of the movement is a very different question. Because Communist Party heads the liberation movement in China, it does not mean it's a *working class* liberation movement. It becomes a national liberation movement of the Chinese *people* under the leadership of the Communist party. In Vietnam, it becomes the liberation struggle of the Vietnamese under the leadership of the Communist Party specially after 1944-45. In Cuba it became a national liberation movement, headed by a party which was by no definition a Communist party (they did not even claim so and the Communist Party opposed them). They became Communist only after Cuba became revolutionary and they nationalised the sugar industry. Of course, Castro was some kind of a Marxist, so was Che Guevara much earlier, but they were not communists nor did they claim that they were establishing Communism, or Socialism. We've asked this question particularly from subalterns as to please tell us what is the Chinese movement — is it subaltern or elite? Was Castro's movement elite or subaltern? That is why we rightly predicted that subalterns will not be able to go anywhere and write a history of any country. For example, they have not written any history of the Indian national liberation struggle. They have not written a history of the Indian peasant movement. You can always take up some little thing and write. Sooner or later, when you are faced with major questions you break up. And they have broken up. They talk of tribal movements, now these are led by tribal chiefs. Are tribal chiefs subalterns or elite? This question is totally evaded by Ranjit Guha in his *Elementary Consciousness*. But even he has written about the 19th century and not the modern movements. He replies that the modern peasantry will also be fighting like indigo rebels — which is rubbish, to use a non-polite word, because nobody in his senses can claim this. Let them write a history of the peasant movement from 1947. They cannot. Satyanand Saraswati is one of their heroes. He is an elite, a swami, a bhoomihar, a brahmin, a landed-person. Is he not an elite? As much an elite as Mahatma Gandhi or Babu Rajendra Prasad. May be less in money but class-wise the same. They can only write about this little thing or that. Nobody in the world has thought of writing subaltern history of the Chinese revolution except Americans. Americans in the heyday of MacCarthyism did write this type of history about the Russian revolution and they said Lenin was an elitist. They said that the Bolshevik Party was a party of elites, and that they imposed revolution upon the Russians. They gave up the attempt to theorise this way because MacCarthyism died in the 50s. Friendship between America and China came and academicists also gave it up.

Now in India from the beginning of the 19th century, in fact even from the middle of the 18th century, colonialism is the dominant reality — colonial economic domination, political domination, cultural domination. Even now I doubt if any work deals with colonial cultural domination. The danger is if you don't notice cultural domination you miss the truth; but if you notice it in a simplistic fashion you may come up with Tagore being the spokesperson of cultural domination, Bankim being the instrument of cultural domination.

There is no aspect of Indian life which was not gradually penetrated by colonialism. This is the dominating reality. Unless one understands this dominating reality in all its complexity, one is not able to understand, from your literature point of view, too. This does not mean that it has to come into analysis when you talk of poet A, B or C. The phrase I use is to be a constant backdrop, against which you have to see other things. It may not even figure in your writing. I think it would be boring if you write on dance or literature and all the time you bring in colonialism. If one sees it that way, then one realises that to free India of colonial domination — economic, political, social, cultural — was essential before the Indian people could start rejuvenating themselves. If one accepts that colonialism is the dominating reality then very clearly freeing India from colonial domination is the other major reality. How is the job done? How well is it done? How badly is it done? What are its weaknesses, strong points? They have to be the very stuff of which the historian has to write. And in a way, I am not talking about the literary part of it but that the ideological content of the 19th and 20th century literature would also reflect this reality. What is the relationship of that literature to colonialism and anti-colonialism? What we call national movement is anti-colonialism. The issue is complicated by the fact that the struggle is not only of the people against colonial domination but simultaneously there are other dominations going on. There is class domination, caste domination. There is domination of the young by the old. There is gender domination. The fact is that there are all sorts of dominations and inequalities and exploitations. They are linked to colonialism, though they are autonomous, too. Simultaneously there has to be a struggle against them. The real question is: How do you relate these two struggles, the struggles for all forms of exploitation with our dominant struggle against colonial domination? It's that which makes the movement vibrant, controversial, makes different ideological trends come and fight each other. This happens the world over. Every national liberation movement has a great deal of struggle. Of course, there are different answers. "Forget about all other exploitations, we are fighting the main enemy. We'll deal with all these other questions afterwords. Fighting for all of them together will only divide the people." But then there is also what I would call the sectarian answer, the Indian Communist answer: "You have to fight against both at the same time," which in practice means fighting more against other contradictions than the colonial contradiction. In 1936, in China Mao Tse Tung proposed that they should join hands with the butcher Chiang Kai Shek because they had to fight Japan. He said that land-lords in China must not be attacked anymore, capitalism must not be attacked anymore. He did not say so after 45, but only when China was threatened by Japan. In other words this is the real problem for any movement and it is also for us as historians.

I am not in a position to speak on literature. I have read literature off and on but I have very little sensitivity. I only see the ideological content of literature. I am not able to see the other aspects. As it is, social and political contradictions would find reflection in literature too. In Prem Chand you find this question of conflicts all the time, which is the primary conflict and which is the secondary? How to reconcile the two? He also criticises the nationalist leaders because he can see clearly that they are not doing anything about the exploitation of the peasant women or other oppressed sections. He is also able to see the other side and therefore constantly shifts attention from one side to the other. This is the reason why national liberation movements are national movements. They have to become the dominant reality for the understanding of our recent history. This means that you have to deal firmly with this aspect and that other aspects, particularly those related to literature would have to be seen in this context.

But isn't that also because the reality of today to a large extent is making one review one's perspective of history and that was how we had phrased the first question that the politics of today are in some ways perhaps also one of the major reasons why one goes back to the questions of colonialism and the rise of nationalism to see where the germs of the conflicts today have been sown and that in some ways goes and redefines one's understanding and perspective of nationalism and colonialism?

In several ways, but the fact is that major writing on colonialism, on modern Indian history abroad and also unfortunately in India, is trying to argue that colonialism didn't exist or that it was a very minor feature. For example, in the Cambridge Economic History of India, Vol. 2 the word "colonialism" does not figure, as if it didn't exist. Even with the subaltern historians it is more or less missing. For us the Indian historians it can never be so unless you are dominated culturally and economically by the west. Imperialism is still a very dominant reality in the world. It may not take the old shape but basically the world is still divided among those — call it the 1st world, call it whatever. Walter Stein calls it the core of the centre. We are still the periphery. Constantly ideology is going to reflect this division. Of course, reflection is never that imperialist ideology is reflected in British universities and anti-colonial ideology in our universities. Just as anti-colonial ideology finds some reflection in the universities there — though very little, more in U.S.A. than in Britain (since British universities are highly controlled). Do you know that British universities never produced till 1945 a single thesis critical of colonialism in any country — India, China, Africa, anywhere?

When we talk about colonialism vis-a-vis nationalism, is it not that the principle of domination or hegemony gets strengthened in the other areas that you have been talking about — don't they get strengthened in a post-independence phase?

The very principle of hegemony is that those who are dominated must also accept your ideological outlook. In historiography, as also in other social sciences — I assume in literary criticism — the imperialist trends in ideology also find reflection here. There are various channels through which British and American universities try to acquire hegemony here. One of them is patronage. Our academics, especially younger ones, feel greatly attracted to go abroad. Still anti-colonial outlook finds some reflection in Britain or U.S.A. or Australia or France. Similarly, their dominating ideology is found here. The divide is intellectual rather than national.

Let's redefine the question. We have a certain structure established within colonialism or imperialism. Now what happens is that after independence somebody from within the tribe, the country itself, rises to the same kind of position and the principle of exploitation or hegemony does not break down. We have something called Black apartheid in Africa and we have people being critical of the Congress ideology in the post-independence era.

There is a very big difference. The principle of exploitation becomes different though exploitation continues. Colonial domination is different from class domination. One can't say that Czarism continues in Soviet Union because a different pattern of dominance emerges there also. In my view even in China there is a pattern of domination but I any day prefer that to what was there before. At the same time, I don't appreciate the lack of democracy there. In India, too, we are no longer suffering from colonial economic domination but from class domination. And some of the earlier dominations like class-exploitation, gender-domination etc. continue. Some of these acquire a new colouring, a new content and also new power. For example, the bourgeoisie was not the main exploiting group in India before 1947. After independence, however, it has increasingly become the main dominating and exploiting group. Therefore, one of the tasks of the historian and social scientist is to both see the exploitation and its changing character. This becomes very difficult in India because we still are threatened by imperialist domination, we still have all forms through which imperialist domination continues. Simultaneously we have got rid of certain kinds of imperialist domination. How to relate ourselves to this complex reality? It is a continuing job. Each generation has to do its own continuous analysis of society and try to find their own ways and means to deal with problems. One of the weaknesses of the Indian Leftists is that they came to certain conclusions in 1951 and they are still continuing with them. CPM had an analysis of India in 1964. That is not wrong. What is wrong is that they still think it's valid in 1991, twenty seven years later — as if History does not change till they come to power. They have now been in power in Bengal for fourteen years as a state government and yet they have made no analysis of what that means for the Indian society. What is their own role in Bengal in the last fourteen years? How are they relating to these different exploitations? They have not even dared to ask the questions. In answer to your question, one must constantly examine as to which are the hegemonic forces and what is the nature of their hegemony. BJP is not going to bring back feudalism. They would also strengthen capitalist sections of society and yet we have to differentiate between Congress domination and BJP. This has to be done on the basis of political ideology and not class domination. Therefore, simple analysis would have to be shelved and very complex analysis made. This is where history can be helpful. We can then see how communalism and such other trends developed in India and which social forces encouraged them. Then I can show that Hindu communalism — BJP, is supported more by small bourgeoisie and according to some analysts it is to be welcomed because it is not representing the big bourgeoisie. In Bihar I can show that the big landlords are with the Janata Dal or Congress, not BJP. Would that make BJP more respectable or better or even equal?

But today in the context of what is happening on the electoral front there has been a movement towards unification of political forces. Especially in so far as BJP is concerned, nationalism and communalism are ceasing to remain separate words. The two trends have supposedly joined forces.

Sorry, nationalism and communalism have not joined forces but your question for me is at the heart of contemporary political situation. The whole point of my analysis was that nationalism in our country was not an ideology of the bourgeoisie or the landlords or peasantry or working class, just as national liberation movement is not based on one single class or is not the ideology of a class. Nationalism could be the instrument not only of national liberation but also social liberation. It could also be the instrument of class domination. Nationalism is what you put in it. Today in India nationalism means the unity of the Indian people. The real point is not that communalism and nationalism are coming together but that BJP is trying to appropriate nationalism and say true communalism is nationalism. The great danger is that if we do not fight back ideologically and politically, they will appropriate nationalism. In our society whichever political formation appropriates nationalism acquires electoral success — nationalism still being a dominant reality in our society. Whenever I attack RSS, it's always for two reasons — they are in my opinion, anti-nationalism and anti-Indian culture. But they are reaching out to millions of people — through shila pujan and all. This is where the fight has to be and we must not permit them to appropriate nationalism. One of our jobs is to delink them from nationalism and Indian culture. All the great writers have constantly fought for nationalism and Indian culture. We have to learn a great deal from our writers.

If we accept pan-nationalism as a unifying force, problems connected with religion, race, region, language, etc. may emerge. We have already seen lots of tensions around us. They continue growing. How do we cope with this?

I see the Naga problem as different from the Punjab problem. We have to realise that certain aspects of life are based upon historical development. For instance India can never be a unilingual country. We must also accept that we have immense cultural diversity, immense geographical diversity. I don't accept the race bit. We are different regions, different cultural zones, different languages. The Indian people's unity has to be based on an acceptance of this diversity. Africa got divided because of too many differences. In a small tiny country like Mozambique, with a population of one crore only, there are seventeen tribes speaking seventeen languages. They consciously accepted Portugese as their official language because otherwise they would have fought tooth and nail as to whose language should become the official language. Guinea has a population of one million and yet they have had problems because there are two or three groups there. Therefore, we should accept diversity as a basic principle. This is one type of diversity. Linguistic diversity can be accommodated by accepting linguistic identity. Religious identity also can be accepted but only for religious purposes. Some tensions arise in India out of the very diversity. The difficulty is that those who are for diversity want too much and those who are against diversity give too little. What is required is a process of adjustment. Also, there is no harm in some struggle, what Mao would call struggle in the camp of the people — non-antagonistic struggle. However, communalism is different. It does not say there should be religious freedom or religious equality. It says that people following a particular religion have the same political, economic and other interests. This is very different. Coming to language, can we say that the interests of Telugu speaking people are different from those of the rest of Indians? Communalism is an illegitimate expression of India's diversity. It does not want religious diversity to remain, but that communalism and religion should determine your political, economic and cultural identities. This creates divisiveness, not tension. The two are different. I sharply differentiate between the linguistic, communal and regional problem. For example, Orissa is less developed. My own area, Himachal Pradesh, used to be less developed. Bihar is under-developed. Now Jharkhand — its problem is partly cultural. These problems of lesser or greater development can be solved through struggle and negotiations. That's how Gurkhaland problem was solved. But communal problem cannot be solved in this manner.

Is Communalism some kind of manifestation of colonialism?

Not colonialism. It is some form of fascism because it asserts an identity based on religion. It also sees religion as the totality of identity. In a multi-religious society, it suggests domination. If one accepts that Hinduism defines your totality of interests, then it means that your totality of interests are opposed to the interests of the Muslims. It suggests that there is total antagonism between Muslims and Hindus. Linguistic identity does not suggest that. Telugu language and its culture does not come in clash with Tamil in any way. There is no question of one being opposed to the other.

Before Independence, the colonial power tried to encourage communal tension in the country.

Yes, but they tried to encourage linguistic tension also. They failed. They tried to encourage caste-tension. But because they tried to encourage communalism, it does not mean communalism is colonialism. They used communalism to try and divide Indian society. They tried to create caste-tensions also. They are the fathers of the policies that V.P. Singh has adopted from Rajni Kothari — divide Indian society along caste-basis. The real divide is class and not caste.

But where nationalism is concerned, the term secularism has come under severe strain specially in today's politics. Nationalism linked with secularism is one of the most debated and criticised topics of today.

Only the communalists, whether Hindu, Muslim or Sikh, constantly question secularism or its relationship with nationalism. Others accept secularism as a positive principle.

Isn't it a frightening fact that the secular voice is being drowned to a very large extent by the communal voice?

True, this is the major danger today, However, that does not indicate any weakness in secularism, it shows the increasing ideological weakness of the Indian people. They are not able to meet and argue out this challenge.

Should'nt nationalism be defined along secular lines?

That has always been so. Nationalism has always opposed the communal definition and adopted a secular definition.

But what are the contents of this nationalism which is now going to form a counter-force to the communal concepts.

Nationalism of the Indian national movement said that in a multi-religious society politics should be delinked from religion and that there should be no discrimination among Indian citizens on the basis of religion. Instead, everybody should have the freedom to practise his or her own religion. This is the only possible definition of secularism. This in fact was the definition given to nationalism by the Indian National Movement. It is precisely this which communalism, both Muslims communalism led by Jinnah and Hindu communalism led by RSS and Hindu Mahasabha, has been challenging. First before 1947, Gandhi and Nehru repeatedly said that in secularism people have every right to be atheists also. Gandhi, an atheist, commenting on the new pledge of Independence said "It is a good pledge but I can't adopt it because I don't believe in God." Gandhi cut out the phrase "by the grace of God." Nehru used to very often say that freedom of religion means also the freedom to oppose religion.

But today the tension is also being generated by the difference between minority communalism and majority communalism.

In fact minority communalism and majority communalism are the same ideology. Just as fascism was the same ideology whether it was in Italy, Japan or Germany. It is not racially linked. Similarly communalism is a single ideology. Communalism as an ideology says that the totality of your secular interests — political, social, cultural, are determined by the religion to which you belong and that interests of people following one religion are opposed to the interests of people following another.

Hasn't the problem come about because secularism is slightly more lenient in its view of minority communalism than in the way it opposes majority communalism?

This is a different question. What you ask now is about the weaknesses that secularists in India have been showing. One of the grounds on which Hindu communalists attack us is that we are soft towards minority communalism. There is some truth in this because secularists have not always been as critical of minority communalism as of majority communalism. Two things here. This is in my writings. The main danger to India today comes from Hindu communalism because only majority communalism can impose fascism. I have even said that minority communalism can at most take a part of Punjab, but only Hindu communalism can destroy the whole Indian society. Therefore it is the major threat. But minority communalism is also very dangerous because it is bad for the minority and it encourages majority communalism. One reason why secular people adopted this view was out of a very decent motive. Nehru wrote: "I agree that Muslim communalism is more strident, more extreme," but he also said that minorities are afraid. In any society, any type of minority will suffer psychologically from fear because of the fact of their being a minority. He said it is for the majority to try and remove the fear of the minority. Therefore, in his own politics in the 50s he criticised minority communalism also. But what happened was that for electoral reasons increasingly Muslims were sought to be used as a vote bank by Congress and by other political parties and they thought if they criticised Muslim communalism, they may not vote for them as a bank. In this way they tried to cater to minority communalism. Its most naked, open form came with the Shah Bano Bill, when Rajiv Gandhi tried to appease the Muslim communalists by passing the Shah Bano Bill. Then came V.P. Singh who tried to appease them in every possible way, including running away from the solution he had offered for Ramjanambhoomi, which in my view was the best solution at that moment of time. But he ran away out of fear of Shahi Imam. But one must differentiate between what you are saying and Hindu communalism. What Hindu communalists say is that secular people are pro-minority. According to a survey of Kerala, 38% of Hindus feel that they are second class citizens. Their propaganda is so successful. While the fact is that there has been no appeasements of Muslims or minorities. What you have had is appeasement of Muslim communalism. And because you have appeased Muslim communalism, you have also tried to counter it by appeasing Hindu communalism. This is what Rajiv Gandhi did in '87 and '89. First, the Shah

Bano Bill, then Shilanyas. This is what V.P. Singh did, on the one hand there was Shahi Imam and on the other Rath yatra of Advani. A TV film was shown on Din Dayal Upadhyaya, who is nobody except an RSS ideologue. I am told that when Doordarshan people refused, the PM ordered that it must be shown. It was to appease Advani. The appeasements go together. Similarly you appease Sikh communalism in Punjab and then Hindu communalism. By appeasing them you encourage both. Therefore if the criticism is that the secularists in India have tended to appease or at least not been so critical of Muslim communalism as they should have been, then, I think it's correct. But the sentiment behind this was healthy — that a minority does deserve to have its fears removed. Nehru in '52-53, when he moved the Hindu code Bill, wanted to have a uniform civil code because Directive Principles say so. But he also explained in letters to Chief Ministers that he excluded Muslim women because those were the post-partition years. We must understand that during the partition period, Muslims had voted for Pakistan and a large number of Hindus had been killed in West Pakistan. Large numbers of Muslims had been killed here also. Muslims who went to Pakistan created communal opinion in Pakistan and Hindus who came here created communal opinion here. There was a great deal of communalism after '47, much more than today. Muslims were not getting jobs here, they could not get houses on rent. One of my friends, a very secular person came back from USA and took a job with one of the voluntary agencies in Delhi. He could not get a house here because he was Muslim. In the end he had to settle in Philippines. Muslims were not in the army, the civil services, the police, not in any private jobs. They were discriminated against everywhere. Consequently, Nehru said that if I now pass this bill then Muslims will say that in India we have no future. Nehru's choice therefore, was either to pass the Hindu code bill for Hindu women only or to wait for 20 years when Muslims would also be ready. He decided not to wait and passed the Hindu code bill. Many historians criticised Nehru. Maybe he was wrong, but his motives were good.

There's one part of the question we seem to have left out — how come the epicentres of all these major agitations have been confined to the North?

Not true. The Dravida separatist movement which was simultaneously casteist and separatist was very strong in Tamil Nadu in the early 50s. Similarly, communalism in its hardened form is found in Kerala. Some people say that in Kerala, Congress is nothing but a coalition of communal forces — Catholic communalism, Nair communalism, casteism. Only it does not take the form of Hindu communalism, but it is communalism, and Muslim League is a powerful force there, especially in the Muslim areas. Why communalism takes this form is North India is because minorities are found in large proportions in the North. One reason why communalism was dormant in the 50s was that Muslims, having fought for Pakistan, were in a weak position, politically and psychologically. But gradually, as the new generation of Muslims came, they had no guilt feeling that they had fought for Pakistan. Why should a Muslim young man born in '35 or '40s feel guilty? Hindu communalism was not able to get more than seven percent votes till the elections of 1989 when both the communists and Janata Dal helped them indirectly or directly. But till then Hindu communalists were a very minor force as fascists in Italy who had around eight percent votes. Seven-eight percent votes any mad man can get in a democracy. But a major reason why communalism is so powerful in the north is that, partially, communalism was born in north, both among Hindus and Muslims, and that as an ideology it has existed for 100 years. Ideologies once born don't die out easily. They have to be combated every day. They are like long-term germs. You have to cleanse them out inch by inch which nobody has done so far. One of my major criticisms of the Left is that it has carried on no campaign against communalism. They are secular, the only fully secular force in India, but they have not carried out any cleansing programme, thus causing the communal ideology to stay in the North. Secondly, in spite of Muslims being small in number in the south, communalism is now growing there also. ABVP has been a major presence in Andhra universities for 30-35 years. In Karnataka, you will see this time BJP will grow. In Kerala, they got seven percent votes in District Council elections, which is the same as they got all over India. Bengal was free from them but now they are growing again in Bengal. If communalism was only a North Indian phenomenon, we could contain it. But it may become and is in fact becoming an all India phenomenon. Most of the trade unions in Bangalore are controlled by Bhartiya Mazdoor Sangh, and you have it in a very powerful form in Kerala. For example, there is Nayyar communalism, Ezwa communalism, now Hindu communalism, Muslim communalism, Catholic Christian communalism; all these are very powerful. They have maintained their growing rate. The movement against the communist government in '59 was led by Catholic communalism. That is what gave it a mass base. The communist government of '59 was virtually overthrown by a mass movement which was led by the Catholic bishops and they gave the cry — "Religion in danger."

There are many reasons for the growth of Hindu communalism. One is the respectability they got in '89, being the indirect allies of Left and Janata Dal. Secondly, they were able to get hold of a religious issue. Communalism never becomes a mass force unless it is allied to some emotional issue like religion. Jobs, reservations etc. can only catch the middle class, not the masses. They have now got a religious issue and we did not do anything when they were getting hold of this. In 1984, they started Ramjanambhoomi. We became aware of the issue in '87. Even then we did nothing. They did Shila pujan, but what did we do? Did we go to the same mohallas and say that shila pujan is spreading communalism? Organising seminars in universities is one thing and talking to an audience of ordinary masses in a mohalla is another.

Given the kind of complex forces at work, particularly where the Indian historians are concerned — what are the tools of analysis that they use? Do they have a certain kind of indigenous theoretical position which is different from the one used by the western historians or are they still tied largely to the western tools of analysis.

There are two things. Firstly, theoretical frameworks and tools are not western or eastern. They are international. They may find birth in one place. Secondly, what is wrong is not the use of western tools by Indian historians or Indian tools by western historians. What is wrong is an unthinking adoption of western constructs and frameworks which are born out of particular societies, social structures and classes and their unthinking, mechanical application. If the same frameworks are analysed and adopted or adopted keeping in mind the Indian situation, I don't see anything wrong in it. That applies to literary criticism as well as to history. What is wrong is that something becomes fashionable there, and we get it here after a few years. The tragedy is that by the time we adopt it, it has already gone out of fashion. I have seen here among Marxists. Gramsci came and it took years to master Gramsci. By the time people had become Gramscians, Althusser became popular. As they mastered Althusser, Foucault came. By the time they became Foucauldians, there came deconstruction. Now they are deconstructionists. I think basically we've got rid of colonial economic domination, except to the extent that we are a part of the world-system and that the developed part of the world exploits the under-developed. But cultural and ideological domination is very different. It takes hundreds of years to have cultural domination. Unfortunately, we are dominated culturally by the developed western countries. Part of that domination is in the form of uncritical adoption of trends that emerge there. They may or may not be useful for us. Some of those trends are the result of the continuation of imperialist ideology. They are aspects of hegemonisation. Some others are a product of typical social, even intellectual conditions. In France, they have an institute for the study of French resistance. This institute started in 1940 and ended in 1945, with nearly 100 faculty members and a full journal which continued researching on Resistance. If they wanted to go further into details of the French Revolution they could easily do so. But we have not even made a study of our national movement which was as revolutionary and historically as significant as the French Revolution. Can we go into those macro-questions which the French take up? They can go to macro-questions because of the work going on in micro-questions. The same applies, I assume, to literature. There is also the question of resources, they have got Church records. They have got a cold climate. Anything written in the 14th or 15th century is preserved. We have no Church records. Neither our birth nor our death takes place in a Church — we burn our bodies. If there is anything written the monsoon destroys it. Above all, I feel that micro-questions can only be asked when macro-questions have been answered to a certain extent. After that, micro-questions can deepen the macro. But in our country most micro-questions have not been asked so far partially because of shortage of intellectual resources. Unfortunately, we have very few researchers in history. I think the same would be true of literary criticism.

Earlier you said that the subaltern approach is not on, the elitist approach is also not on. Then, given our historical reality and going back to the 19th century in terms of the freedom movement itself, what constitutes or should constitute the epicentre of our historical readings? What should we be working on, given the diversity of our situation? Given the colonialist and nationalist situation, if we can use that as a binary opposition, what should constitute the focal point or the epicentre of our historical research?

Let me link the two questions. What about today's world? How does it enable us to look at the past? We will find that a great deal of our negative features are not merely the result of colonial domination. A great deal of what is positive in India is associated with our freedom struggle. However, what is negative in India today is also the result of the manner in which the freedom struggle was fought, the manner in which its ideology, its politics evolved. These questions go on changing with today's world. Thirty years ago, I believed that non-violence was at the heart of the weakness of the National Movement. Today I would not say that; today I accept that perhaps non-violent social transformation was possible and desirable and I would therefore look for its weaknesses in some other direction. Today I would see non-violence as a significant force of the freedom movement. In this way, contemporary situations force us to ask new questions. The fact that we still are living in a world of imperialism, our focal point still has to be the study of colonialism and the National Movement and the relationship these two had to the development of Indian society and economy. For example, the formation and role of the middle class. The positive and negative roles of the middle class have still not been fully analysed. I believe that the overall Marxist framework is the only framework that can help us analyse any society. Only, it has not to be mechanical Marxism but Marxism which is constantly developing. Till now historians have only said that they applied Marxism wrongly. In my view the point was never to apply Marxism in India correctly but to develop Marxism in Indian conditions. In my opinion, this is what went wrong in socialist countries. They did not develop Marxism along with efforts at building socialism, rather they tried to apply it. Anything needs to be properly deepened, properly developed. Let us take the example of non-violence. Marxists have been of the view that non-violence is an ideology of the ruling classes and that violent liberation is the only possible way for the masses to fight ruling class subjugation. I think it was true in the 19th century. I don't see how Lenin could have liberated the Soviet Union from Tsarist Russian structure with non-violence. But increasingly in the 20th century, the very manner in which Eastern Europe has been now liberated shows the strength of non-violence. The fact is that in social sciences, including literature, non-Marxists were also developing. Marxists had a closed mind to them. They refused to learn. The most classic example was that Cybernetics was declared to be a bourgeois science. I think one has to have complete openness, complete absorption, complete development and so on. Marxism in my view has two great things: one, it is interdisciplinary — it is the only holistic principle which tries to analyse society in its totality. Many Marxists don't do it unfortunately, but Marxism is the only way to grasp the totality of reality. As E.H. Carr put it: There is multi-causation but it does not mean that all the causes are equal. There is a hierarchy of causations. I think Marxism is the one way of looking at reality which recognises the multiplicity of forces working and simultaneously tries to grasp as to which at any moment is the more primary causation. It may go on changing its notion of primary causation, but it constantly looks for hierarchy of causations. The other thing is that class struggle as visualised by Marxism is one of the profoundest truths of society. This is being increasingly accepted by all social sciences. Social division and class division do affect, not necessarily determine, all areas of life. But I think Marxism is like a sharp weapon — it tends to cut those who use it much more often, specially if it is not used in a very careful manner. For example, declaring nationalism to be bourgeois, the Indian National Movement was defined by Palme Dutt and many other Marxists to be a bourgeois movement. It may or may not have been but this was done without proper analysis. Similarly communalism is just declared to be the instrument of the feudal classes. Where are the feudal classes in India? Yet communalism is growing very fast. Tomorrow, the big bourgeoisie may support BJP but that does not mean it would become an instrument of the big bourgeoisie. That does not help us at all. How does it help us to say that fascism was the instrument of the ruling classes in Germany? One reason why we failed to fight it was that we termed communalism the instrument of the ruling class. That alone does not help unless we further analyse why it is making an appeal to the people. In my view, we Marxists have ignored that it is the petty bourgeoisie which is associated with communalism. We have neither been willing to criticise the petty bourgeoisie nor have we been willing to work among them.

Let's go back to that question of western theoretical models and their application in the Indian situation. Where exactly are you pinpointing the problem of applying western theories to Indian reality? One, you did take up the issue vis-a-vis the French school. What about...

Not French school because there are many French schools.

No, but what about certain other theories that are emerging, whether of Foucault or Derrida, where they are questioning the basic structure of reality itself, where they are asking a lot of questions about what constitutes historical reality and the contending forces....

Though I am not myself a deconstructionist or anything — I don't even understand it, yet I am not at all opposed to people understanding Foucault and trying to learn from him and applying in scientific terms his way of understanding historical reality, trying to see Indian history in that light. I am opposed to its being done uncritically. If a scholar believes and understands Foucault and believes that his notions of power, for example, are very relevant to understanding Indian reality and history, he has every right to pursue it that way because truth emerges out of contention. In current theory, this new idea of power has emerged and should be seriously considered. Take, for instance, a critique of socialist countries that you may not have economic exploitation there but exploitation of another kind does exist which operates through bureaucratic power. I still do not accept the argument, but I think we should have paid attention to what was being said and tried to see to what extent such notions and theories were applicable to the reality of the socialist countries.

I think one must learn deeply. Our strength is we know English, our weak point is that consequently we ignore all other foreign languages. I have been trying to persuade my students for twenty years now in JNU to pick up other languages. I am too old and I do not know languages. We do not know what is happening in Mexico, in Spain, in Italy. If New Left publishes two or three books from Italy, then Marxists come to know about it. But if they don't, then I do not know what has happened in Italian Marxism for the last forty-five years. Not many books have been translated. A lot of work must have gone on. In J.N.U. we made one Indian language compulsory for every M.A. student. Every M.A. student, therefore, studies one Indian language other than his mother tongue. The same holds true for M.Phil. But in twenty years, we haven't produced a single student who has used that knowledge of language to read literature or history or anything else. Students don't take it seriously, they pass the examination, get an A and they forget the language. Isn't this a major weakness that we can't read other Indian languages even, leave aside other world languages? As a result, we become dependent upon translations, which reach us years later.

Is that one of the major areas where historians are looking for meaningful answers? Are we saying historical reality is influenced by translation?

No, I am not saying that because I don't know enough about translating. What I say is that either books are not available because they are not translated or that sometimes they are translated very late. I am making a minor point, not going into the profundity of the act of translation. My problems as a historian are different. If a student wants to study the National Movement he faces questions like: (a) what was the level of participation of people in the movement, and particularly which section of the people participated? (b) why did they participate? (c) what was the ideological content of their participation? That is, if it was a popular movement then what was the people's role in it? Not only in the sense of who went to jail and who demonstrated. We know what Gandhi thought, what Nehru thought, what the people thought. Questions to be asked are: Why did they participate? What was their understanding of colonialism? What did they expect from the movement? Why did they go to jail? Why did they demonstrate? Why did they feed the freedom fighters? This is an area which in the 1920s came to be known as people's history. One of my major criticisms of subaltern historians is that they have been flying under wrong colours. The notion that true history is the history of the people is broadly an idea of Marxism but it is essentially an idea of labourites and Fabians. One of the first appeals for people's history was made by Babu Rajendra Prasad in 1934 that historians must not write the history of kings and rulers and leaders but history of the people. Subalterns are absolutely right when they say that history must above all tell us about the history of the people because it is the people above all who make history. But on what one disagrees with them is the notion that history can only be a history of the common masses, delinked from other aspects. In working out such questions, language becomes important — they cannot be answered without the historian knowing the language. Now a Bengali can write about Bengal but not about Orissa. And I, if I want to write, must know some Indian languages. I think it will be a very narrow history if we say: let Bengalis work on Bengal's history and Punjabis on Punjab and Maharashtrians on Maharashtra. But about foreign languages my point was that the knowledge available, the content available, is available through languages other than English. Even I'd like to know what French historians are thinking and writing about the French revolution. I'd like to read not one or two books translated by someone but their journals at length. This is a major weakness of ours. I find all major scholars — Eric Hobsbawm, Christopher Hill, Wallerstein — they know English, German, French — most of them know Russian, they know Spahish, Portuguese, Italian. They are able to write at a level of profundity which we can never achieve. I cannot. Indians are supposed to be good at languages. I wish Indian scholars would learn foreign languages, at least three. It's not difficult. French you can learn. Italian, Spanish, Portuguese you can learn in no time. At least a good scholar, a good literary critic can.

We talked of Foucault and Derrida. Going outside that, what about writers like Raymond Aron, Braudel — does one concede that they can also contribute to truth? If so, then doesn't our idea of truth — these kind of people are saying something very different from what the mainstream Marxist historians would say — then does'nt our idea of historical truth take a bit of a beating? If we concede that Braudel also is speaking some kind of truth, Georges Duby too, Raymond Aron and Derrida and Foucault too — then what happens to historical truth?

Historical truth is firstly an on-going process — there is no such thing as absolute truth. Braudel has some truth or Foucault has it. We Marxists may have missed — we should never claim to have achieved the absolute truth. That is what was wrong with Marxism. Many of us as young people were attracted to Marxism because it enabled us to have a few formulas which would answer every question. I still remember that I did a course on economic thought and a question came — economic thought from Aristotle to Physiocrats and I applied my Marxism and linked it up with the class structure. My American teacher gave me A — and said, "You are young, so I am not giving you a low grade. This shows that you have read but give it all up." I got my lesson on this from Paul Baran. I did a course with him and he asked me to write a review of Aba Lerner's book. Aba Lerner was a liberal economist who was a socialist and whose first book was on socialism looked at from the liberal position. So I wrote a critique in which I used class and this and that, called him bourgeois, all sorts of things. Paul Baran gave me a C and said "Don't write like this. Who are you to call Aba Lerner all this, what do you know?" I said, "But you have used such words about Aba Lerner in one article." He said, "But I know what I am writing, you don't." The point was that he had read Aba Lerner fully, while I had read a little and was applying my elementary Marxism and accusing him of this and that. The point is simple, if they have also truth — Aron, I think is the most wrong of them all — but even if he has some element of truth, it means we have missed out some aspect of truth and must always accept it if it comes our way. There are always some elements of truth that are missing. If we have to operate in the field of culture or politics, we must have as large a segment of truth on our side as possible.

If we concede that absolute truth does not exist, then what is the validity of any historical narrative?

The extent to which it is able to approach the truth, which means the extent to which it is able to explain reality better.

But wouldn't this reality, this truth...

Despite all these people having all sorts of truth on their side, I still believe that class-analysis is able to grasp reality better than other ways of analysing. Within that I would like to incorporate world systems, imperialism — after all not I, Lenin did that — he was able to incorporate within class-analysis the role of imperialism and say that Gandhi was a revolutionary because he was fighting British forces. He would see that fighting against imperialism was not class struggle, but under particular conditions it was even higher than class struggle. That does not mean that class struggle is not the basic feature of reality but as Althusser, I think, very profoundly says that there can be over-determination even in the role of an individual. Even Rajiv Gandhi, his assassination can help grasp the significance of a particular phenomenon which in the short term or long run may have implications beyond class-analysis.

Again, a somewhat presumptious question - when one writes history, do the conclusions emerge out of the work or is it possible, or does it happen, that conclusions are already there and historical writing becomes a means of proving those conclusions?

Both are wrong positions. Because consciously or unconsciously what a historian does is that he has a framework, hypothesis, a theoretical framework. Theoretical framework means a much more conscious and structured framework. Hypothesis means less structured but it has a framework as the historian tries to gather evidence in the light of that framework. The real problem is not, therefore, this. The real problem is the extent to which the framework is not borne out by the evidence, data. Empirical data and the framework are constantly interacting with each other and a good historian is one who constantly allows this interaction to take place. He is constantly revising his theoretical construct and he is at the same time looking for explanations through his hypothesis. Thirdly he finds lacuna by gathering new evidence either to bolster his hypothesis or to modify it. The problem arises when a historian thinks he is only drawing conclusions from evidence — that means he is not aware of his bias. It's a well-known position. I don't have to say any more on that.

How did a critical view of communist practice emerge in your thinking?

My criticism of the communist movement developed gradually over the years as I began to realise that others used their critique of colonialism better to pursue their politics. On the other hand, communists practised wrong politics. The critique of colonialism was crucial without which you could not lay the foundation of an advanced national liberation struggle. That is why in China, Sun Yat Sen became really great because he accepted their analysis after 1900. Then I applied it here. I realised that the communist movement failed to make any headway since it had not made a critique of contemporary Indian society and economy. Where is the contemporary Indian society and economy? Where is the contemporary critique of Indian economy? — some booklet of Namboodiripad, okay, but there is not a single Marxist work which analyses, or makes a critique of Indian economy as a whole — be it industrial policy, agriculture or trade. The sort of book I have on moderates — anybody can see here is a critique of colonialism. Where is such a critique of contemporary society? I have asked two-three Marxist economists: Why don't you devote ten years and — like Marx — analyse Indian economy? They have not undertaken the task.

You talked of fidelity to evidence. What is evidence? Can one be so absolutist? Is not the idea of evidence different for different historians? And secondly, is not evidence also open to interpretation?

That is why a historian goes with a hypothesis to the evidence. Evidence, as Carr puts it, the data is already the result of somebody's mind. Any data, except archaelogical data which is impartial, all written data is already the product of somebody's mind. Even a government report, newspaper, even census, is the product of somebody's mind. Data is not absolute, it's not God. We have to analyse the data. And that's the importance of hypothesis. Therefore, I say that Marxists can analyse the data better than non-Marxists. A Marxist goes with a much better hypothesis to the data. But a Marxist may not know how to do it, he may do it rigidly, wrongly. But there is no such thing as sovereignty of the data. But simultaneously if there is no sovereignty of data, data can also not be moulded any way you want. It has to be critically assimilated which means it has half a sovereignty, in the sense that you can't violate it either. Then you produce bad history. As I said, proper research is a dialectic between the historian and the data, both are open to change in interpretation. Some data may be used. I think great historians — let's not miss historians like Lefebre or Christopher Hill — are able to interpret data in such a fashion that others dare not challenge their basic interpretation, through they may try to further change and develop it.

On the question of data, you have the "mentalite" tradition which talks about private letters, about wills — all these things constituting data or evidence. Would you really go along with that?

All types of data are historical data — letters certainly, wills, of course — it tells you a great deal of the person who has written the will and of the society in which he lived. The only thing is that it's less now than before, people thought that a speech by a leader is meant for public, but if he writes a letter to somebody then he is telling the truth. This is not true. A private letter is also an ideological document. This is what the Cambridge school does — it says this is the noting of the Viceroy, it's not for the public, therefore it is pure.

From a historian's point of view, what about a literary work as a historical document?

This is one of the things that we have been trying to promote. Even this time in one of my seminars I asked two people to do research on Left Urdu novel of 1937 to 1947 and tell us something about the society of that period. It requires great skill and provides knowledge not only of the life of the writer but of the period in which it is written.

What are the difficulties involved?

The writer is writing as an individual, it's his experience, his understanding, it's not as if he is telling the truth, it's only his understanding. If it is a great artist it is different. Great artists have a way of understanding the reality which is not necessarily through the rational process with which we do it. We gather evidence and then say this is exploitation. We will gather evidence of percentage of revenues and find out the level of rent and so on. While a Prem Chand work may be able to understand the nature of exploitation of the peasant by living among them. What Gramsci says is true about a writer also. He says that a political leader has a rational process of understanding reality but there is an intuitive process which makes a leader great. You and I are not leaders but he is because he is able to understand reality. Gramsci says that this aspect one cannot analyse because it is not rational. A social scientist can only analyse the fact which is rational. Why Prem Chand is able to understand Indian reality so well and not somebody else? I don't think you can fully answer that. You cannot say Prem Chand read more government reports or he lived more among the peasants, and so on, because another fellow may have lived more among the peasants. Prem Chand had the capacity to understand. And this is why literature is an important source — it enables us to grasp reality which is not open to us through documents because it is the product of a mind, a mind that is specially endowed to grasp the reality. Having accepted that, one has to be careful. It could be partial, it could be a class-view, a view of a caste, of a person's psychology — a result of his frustrations in love or what. There are so many factors — we cannot accept it as truth. Nevertheless, it's a major source of understanding reality. But one cannot understand without understanding the author and his time.

You have studied the 19th century history. Can you take an example from 19th century literature? Did you take any help from literary works in understanding the Indian society of that period?

I am afraid I have only tried to understand what a writer has ideologically said and its ideological impact on society.

For instance, you have read Ghalib, what are your comments on Ghalib?

Ghalib — the more one reads Ghalib, the more one understands aspects of his life and aspects of human condition.

And about the 19th century?

Yes, about the 19th century India also. As I said his times, his society, but also of human condition as such.

Let's complicate the issues a bit. Suppose instead of taking an accepted major writer or supposedly a big literary figure, we take up a minor author — what would be his status from the historian's point of view — regarding his work as historical evidence.

You see "minor" has two meanings. It can mean — bad writer but also an author who has written little or who has been able to grasp some aspects of reality without being able to translate them properly. It can also mean a writer who is not fully recognised because of paucity of his work or lack or people knowing him. Bad writer apart, however minor a writer — if a historian was to use literature as a source, then he must go to a very large number of writers. That is one reason that I have not used literature at all because it would be dangerous to use Prem Chand or Tagore or Bankim, except in the classroom. Unless one was able to read the contemporaries of Bankim or Prem Chand on a very large scale, I don't think one has a right to use literature as a major source. Then one should have the capacity to link up and grasp. This is where we require a community of thinkers, of researchers. Literature is a very important source, but for me it becomes a source only if my fellow colleagues write and make their analyses available to me. But no one historian or even group can achieve this. I'll give you an example. We have a Penguin book that came out in 1988 written by five-six authors. Two areas are missing in that book. We are conscious of it. Covering India's struggle for independence was the aim. There are chapters on peasant movement, trade-movement, revolutionary terrorists, and so on. There is nothing on the role of culture, not literature but culture as such. Social reform movement — yes, but not literary culture. We were not able to persuade any person, who we believed would be able to write well.

Ram Bilas Sharma would have. His framework is largely acceptable from the radical point of view. Still at the same time, couldn't it be a problem of defining Indian culture itself, because of the complexities in what constitutes Indian culture?

What we wanted was in a narrower frame. What was the anti-imperialist struggle at the cultural level? All of us are hampered by the fact that we don't have the necessary research and expertise in many areas. The Hindi people — who have written many books on the role of Hindi in the anti-imperialist struggle are very poor. I have read two-three books. They tend to make a one to one equation, which is not the way at all.

Conversely, what is the use of history for a literary writer?

Even to understand what one is grasping, one has to know the historical period.

For the writer who is writing, what is the importance of understanding the historical process?

No good writer would rely only upon his intuition, just as no great political leader — Gramsci — would rely upon his own intuition. He would like to increase the area of rationality and decrease that of intuition. Even Gandhi, who used to say that his inner voice told him, said that his inner voice was that which other people called reason. Therefore, it is for people to say fifty years after a writer's death that he arrived at the truth intuitively, but no writer would like to arrive at the truth intuitively. Instead, he would like to understand it. However, intuition plays a role in historical writing also.

A historian, too, would grasp things intuitively. I have said this is true of writers. I think it's true of historians, too. It's one thing common between the two. Whichever period one is writing on, one should be able to live in it. I'll give you a bit of autobiography. My thesis, I wrote its conclusion of twenty-five pages in one sitting in twenty-four hours without sleep. Early in the morning when I wrote the last word, I cried for two hours. I couldn't stop. Instead of being super-happy that I had finished my thesis. My wife consoled me. I had quoted Gokhale in the end and I said, "Gone, these people, I'll never meet them again, I have lived with them for five years. I have known them better than any one else and now they are gone. I miss them, I cry for them." This is what we call empathy. It's a thing common between a historian and a writer. They must have empathy for the period. I cannot write a history of the British administration in the same way. I have empathy with the national leaders. I cannot empathise with Curzon, I can totally criticise him. But I must get under his skin and understand what he is before I criticise him. Ilya Ehrenburg spoke in Delhi University in his hey-day after de-Stalinisation. He had written his last famous work, critical of the Stalin period. He was asked many questions. He said, "No writer can write about a character without getting under his skin. That is why you'll find that prostitutes, drunkards, dacoits are very beautifully portrayed in my books. When I write about them I am able to see myself." He said, "You can see all my novels. I am never able to portray a traitor because I have tried my level best but I have never been able to see myself as committing treason. How do I betray my country?" He said, "I have put in traitors but they are cardboard characters — they are intellectual constructs." The historian also has to grasp the period. For that he requires reading, data, but he also requires in a way an intuitive capacity.

Since we are on this area of interrelationship between history and fiction, can we move on to a kind of fiction that bases itself on historical details, like Manohar Malgaonkar's The Devil's Wind, or Tom Gibson's A Soldier of India. These are novels that are really historical presentations. Of course, the writers' points of view are there — the writers are really trying to write in terms of what constitutes evidence in history.

The question is — is the writer really able to recreate what is history? Because quite often, the historical novelist uses historical characters and narrative but characters bear no relationship to the reality of that period.

But some have tried quite successfully.

That would mean that they would be very profoundly read in that period. I can't imagine anyone writing about say the revolt of 1857 or the Indigo peasants revolt. I have read some novels of the peasant revolt. Krishan Chander is a good example when he writes about Telangana. He does not know the a, b, c, of the Telangana structure, peasant movement, etc., but he writes as a revolutionary. For him the peasant revolution is nothing but his construct. He can't come to grips with reality. Telengana is a contemporary period. But even about the past, a person would have to be very deeply read.

Why wouldn't a historical novelist be termed a historian, why would he be called a fiction-writer. His characters are historical figures, he is basing his facts on happenings that took place. He has done a great deal of research and reconstructed a happening. Then, why isn't he given the status of a historian?

He is not a historian because after researching, he has let his imagination create events, which is not true of a historian. A historian does not create events, he is bound by them. For example, a novelist writing on Gandhi in Africa may do a far better job but he will be creating Gandhi and what is happening in Africa from his imagination.

I would say that a historical novelist may get at the reality but he won't be a historian. Historian writes about things as they were.

But even that is a reconstruction and isn't that marked by a point of view?

Reconstruction bound by evidence, bound by events, by characters, bound by what happened. I say that history is a history of what happened. What happened has to be reconstructed but still it is in a sense what happened. While a historical novelist is only presenting the spirit of the thing, not what happened. He may create a love-affair for Gandhi — and his attitude towards women and sex may come out better than otherwise but as a historian I can't create an affair for him which may become necessary if you want to bring out his relationship with women.

Talking about a historical narrative, isn't there a certain amount of construction involved there too. There is a reference in Ishwari Prashad to Aurangzeb's sitting and meditating even as a child, and the historian asserts that he had a philosophical bent of mind even before he became a ruler. I wonder if that sort of a thing would appear in any historical evidence — wouldn't that amount to creating events.

Very much so. A good historian won't do that and if he does he will make it clear in his writing that this is the evidence on the basis of which he is projecting it. They make it clear that now they are reconstructing just like a fiction-writer. When Ishwari Prasad does that he is not working as a historian at all, unless he has evidence.

Then what you are saying is that a novelist and a historian are both capable of realising truth in their own ways, the truth which is the social truth, the historical truth. But in their methods of depicting it they are radically different.

Only thing is, a novelist writing about contemporary time is very different because there he can even score over the historian — he is living in that period and therefore intuitively grasping the reality. But the historical novelist is different, he is entirely dependent upon the historian for trying to grasp the historical concerns.

Another question. We were earlier discussing personal letters, wills etc. and the author and his fictional writing. Why is it that from a historian's point of view, these wills, etc. are supposed to be documents, while one is not bothered by the existence or non-existence of the authors of those documents. On the other hand as soon as it comes to supposedly fictional works, then one gets bothered about the writers.

You know, if you want to analyse a work of literature, you have to know who the author was, what he was doing, what were his experiences.

It is the same, with historical documents, very much so. For example, whether a note has been put by a Deputy Secretary or a Secretary. That makes a difference. If it's a newspaper report, who is the reporter, etc.

But that would be related more to his status and not necessarily to what that person thinks, what his beliefs were.

No, that also is important. The limitation is if you are writing about a novelist, it's possible and necessary for you to go into it at great length. When I am writing about British policy in the 30s and I am reading accounts of two hundred officials, it's not possible for me to go into the life of each one. But if I am writing about Lord Dufferin or about one official only, then I will go through his life with a toothpick, not just his childhood but even his ancestors. His school, its atmosphere. Suppose you were writing an article on short stories and were covering 30 authors you wouldn't have time to go into the lives of each. Its a question of time, again my point of supportive research comes up there. If we had thousands of historians working, then we would go into all those details. In Britain the history of every village has been written ten times over. Every major official and member of parliament has been researched, but I won't be able to do it here because it isn't possible time-wise, though it should be done.

But aren't there also two different approaches in the understanding of history?

Difference is not of approaches but of the questions you are asking. For some questions you have to go into the personality, for others you don't. The same is true for literary criticism. Suppose you are asking questions about the influence of deconstruction on two contemporary authors, then you will go into their personality, but if the question asked is about the impact a work leaves, you will go into the nature of the work. It is immaterial then whether the writers are young or old, Punjabis or Bengalis, this or that. It's not approaches but the question you are asking. You may argue: The question you are asking would depend on your approach: a particular approach would mean that you ask one type of questions. Historians who believe that individuals play the geatest role in history would ask one type of questions. Those who, like some of us, believe in social forces will ask different types of questions. One of my greatest ambitions is to learn Gujarati to read Gandhi in the original. If I believe Gandhi is more important than I thought, I would study him more thoroughly. If I regard Azad of some importance, I'll read selections of his speeches. If my problem requires giving him still more importance, I'll read all his letters.

(At this point it was mutually decided to conclude the discussion. The possibility of a future dialogue is not foreclosed but left for another time.)

INDEX

A.B.V.P., 139
Advani, 99, 138
Agnew, Jean-Christophe
  "The Consuming Vision of Henry James", 93-21
Ainsworth, 56
Allen, Elizabeth, 92-5
Althusser, 140, 146
Appiah, Kwame Anthony, 108
  "Is the post in postmodern the post in post-colonial ?", 108
Aron, Raymond, 112-113, 145
  Introduction to the Philosophy of History, 112, 113
Arnold, 29
Ashcroft, Bill
  The Empire Writes Back, 109-8
Aurangzeb, 153
Austen, Jane, 55
Azad, Maulana, 155

B.J.P., 99, 100-101, 133, 134, 139
Bakhtin, Mikhail, 57
  Problems of Dostoyevski's Poetics, 57
Ball, Charles, 122-18
Balzac, 20
Baran, Paul, 146
Barthes, Roland
  Image/Music/Text, 96
Batsleer, Janet
  "Gender and Genre: Women's stories", 106
Belsey, Catherine
  Critical Practice, 107
Benjamin, Walter
  Illuminations, 52
Bennett, Tony, 77, 96
  "Text and History", 77
Bersani, Leo
  "The Narrator at Center in The Wings of the Dove", 92-7

Best, G., 50
  Mid-Victorian Britain 1815-1875, 50, 61-12
Bhabha, Homi, 104
  "The other question: difference, discrimination and the discourse of Colonialism.", 104
Bhartiya Mazdoor Sangh, 139
Blake, 36
Bolshevik Party, 129
Book of Job, 97-99, 101
Bradbury, Malcolm
  Forster: A Collection of Critical Essays, 105
Braudel, Fernand, 113, 115, 145
  On History, 113, 115
Brecht, 31
Briggs, Asa,
  "Cholera and Society in the Nineteenth Century", 54, 61-27
Brooke-Rose, Christine
  "The Rhetoric of the Unreal", 101, 102
Bulwer, 56
Butler, 105

C.P.I., 99
C.P.M., 25, 133
Cambridge Economic History of India, 131
Campbell, Colin, 118-19
Carlyle, T., 48
  Selected Essays, 48
Carr, E.H., 142, 148
Castro, 128, 129
Cazamian, Louis, 44
  The Social Novel in England, 1830-1850, 44
Cecil, David, 69
Chander, Krishan, 152
Chandra, Bankim, 129, 150
Chandra, Sarat, 20

INDEX

Chesterton, 69
Chiang Kai Shek, 130
Colby, F.M., 86
   "In Darkest James", 86
Congress, 25, 133, 137
Connerton, Paul
   Critical Sociology, 108
Conrad, Joseph, 97, 101-04
   Lord Jim, 97, 101-04
Cornhill Magazine, 50
Crisp, Peter
   "Essence, Realism and Literature", 109-*10*
Culler, Jonathan
   "Literary Competence", 96
Curtin, Philip D., 120
   Imperialism, 120
Curzon, 105

Derozio, H.V., 39
Derrida, 143, 145
Devi, Mahashweta, 20
Dhagamwar, Vasudha, 101
Dickens, Charles, 21, 41-75
   Bleak House, 51-60
   David Copperfield, 57
   Dombey and Son, 51, 57, 66, 70
   Great Expectations, 51, 60
   Hard Times, 65-75
   Little Dorrit, 60-70
   Nicholas Nickleby, 46
   Old Curiosity Shop, 45
   Oliver Twist, 46, 47, 48, 52, 56,
   Our Mutual Friend, 51, 60, 70
   Pickwick Papers, 46
   The Chimes 44, 51, 52
   The Letters of Charles Dickens, 42-43
Disraeli, 128
Dostoevsky, 69
Drabble, Margaret, 113
Duby, Georges, 122-*12*
Dutta, Michael Madhusudan, 39-40
   Meghnadbadh, 39-40
Dufferin, 154

Eagleton, Terry
   Criticism and Ideology, 93-9, 22
Ehrenburg, Ilya, 151
Eliot, George, 55
Eliot, T.S., 13, 26, 31, 97-101
   Murder in the Cathedral, 97, 99-100, 101
Engels, F., 21, 42, 52
   The Condition of the Working Class in England, 21, 42, 52

Farrell, J.G., 111-23
   The Siege of Krishnapur, 111-23
Flaubert, 66
Forrest, G.W.
   Selections from the Letters Presented in Lucknow and Cawnpore, 1857-58, 116, 118, 119, 121, 122-*18*
Forster, E.M. 14, 97, 104-07
   A Passage to India, 14, 97, 104-07
Fortnightly Review, 53
Foucault, 31-32, 99, 140, 143, 145

Gandhi, Indira, 31
Gandhi, Mahatma, 30, 129, 136, 144, 146, 151, 152, 153, 154
Gandhi, Rajiv, 31, 137, 147
Gates, Henry Lewis
   "Authority, (White) Power and the Black Critic", 108
Germon, Maria, 116, 118
   Journal of the Siege of Lucknow, 116, 118
Ghalib, 149, 150
Ghosh, Sisir Kumar, 38
   "The Future of English Studies in India", 38
Gibson, Tom, 152
   A Soldier of India, 152
Gladstone, 128
Goethe, 20
Gokhale, 151
Goode, John, 92-5
Graff, Gerald
   "The Future of Theory in the Teach-

ing of Literature", 96, 108
Graham, Kenneth
  English Criticism, 61-*31*
Gramsci, 37, 128, 140, 149, 151
Greene, Graham, 15
Guevara, Che, 128
Guha, Ranjit, 129
  Elementary Consciousness, 129

Hafiz, 39
Hardy, Thomas, 21
  Tess, 21
  Mayor of Casterbridge, 21
Havelock, 118
Hill, Christopher, 143, 148
Hilton, Richard, 120
  The Indian Mutiny, 120
Himmelfarb, Gertrude, 44-45
  The Idea of Poverty in England in the Early Industrial Age, 42, 44-45, 52, 60-*4*
Hindu Mahasabha, 136
Hirsch David, 72
  "*Hard Times* and F.R. Leavis", 72
Hobsbawm, E.J., 48-49, 145
  Industry and Empire, 41, 48-49, 60-2, 145
Holloway, John
  "*Hard Times* : A History and a Criticism", 69, 71-72
House, Humphrey
  The Dickens World, 60-*4*
  Household Words, 50, 51
Hull, E.M., 107
  The Sheik, 107
Hutcheon, Linda
  A Poetics of Postmodernism, 106
  Narcissistic Narrative, 107
  Indian Express, 101

Inglis, J.E.M., 116

James, Henry, 55, 77-94
  The American Scene, 89
  The Princess Casamassima, 77
  The Wings of the Dove, 77-94
Jameson, Fredric
  The Political Unconscious, 102
  "The Realist Floor-Plan", 78
Janata Dal, 133, 139, 140
Janata Party, 31
Jinnah, 136
Johnson, 127
Johnson, Samuel, 18, 19
Jones, Gareth Steadman, 49, 50

Kafka, 69
Kappeler, Susan, 77-78
  Writing and Reading in Henry James, 77-78
Karl, Frederick
  Readers' Guide to Joseph Conrad, 102
Kaye, W., 121, 122-*18*
Keats, 26-40
  Endymion, 26
  "Ode to a Nightingale", 26-27, 32, 33-34
  "Ode on a Grecian Urn", 27-28, 32, 34
  "Ode on Melancholy", 28, 34
  "Ode to Autumn", 28-30, 35
Kermode, Frank, 98
  The Genesis of Secrecy, 98
Kinsley, Charles, 42
  Alton Locke, 42
Kipling, Rudyard, 128
Kunte vs. Prabhoo, 101

Lakoff, Robin, 91
  Language and Woman's Place, 91
Lawrence, D.H., 13, 71, 72
Lawrence, Henry, 116, 117
Leavis, F.R., 26, 31, 63-75
  "*Dombey and Son*", 66
  The Great Tradition, 65, 66, 67, 71, 72
Lee, Vernon, 86
  The Handling of Words, 86
Lefebre, 148

INDEX

Lenin, 129, 142, 146
Lerner, Aba, 146
Lukacs, 111

Malgaonkar, Manohar, 152
   The Devil's Wind, 152
Madho, Beni, 120
Mao Tse Tung, 130, 134
Manzoni, Alessandro, 111
   On the Historical Novel, 111
Marx, 128
Masson, Tom, 86
"Mary's Little Lamb. In Different Keys", 86
Mayhew, Henry, 52, 53, 54
   The London Labour and the London Poor, 52, 53, 54
Meredith, 105
Mill, J.S.
   "Article on French Novels", 62-*30*
Milton, 19, 20, 39
Moggach, Deborah, 105-07
   Hot Water Man, 105-07
Mowbray, J.P., 85
   "The Apotheosis of Henry James", 85-86
Mukherjee, Rudrangshu
   Awadh in Revolt, 123-29
Mukherji, Meenakshi, 38
   "Teaching of Literature to a Sub-Culture", 38
Murry, J. Middleton, 26, 30

Namboodiripad, 147
Nehru, 136, 137, 138, 144
Norrman, Ralph, 86
   The Insecure World of Henry James' Fiction, 79, 86, 87

Orwell, 69
Outram, James, 118

Palme Dutt, 143
Perkin, Harold
   The Origin of Modern English Society 1780-1880, 61-*12*
Phillips, Walter C., *Dickens, Reade and Collins: Sensational Novelists*, 61-*31*
Phule, Jyotibha, 101
Polehampton, H.S., 116
Pope, 35
Porter, G.R., 53
   The Progress of a Nation, 53
Prasad, Ishwari, 153
Prasad, Babu Rajendra, 129, 145
Prem Chand, 20, 131, 149, 150

Quarterly Review, 49

R.S.S., 134, 136, 138
Reagan, 31
Ricoeur, Paul, 111, 112
   Time and Narrative, 111, 112, 115
Ritambhara, Sadhvi, 99
Russell, Bertrand, 15

Said, Edward, 34
   Orientalism, 104
Sangari, Kumkum
   "Of Ladies, Gentlemen and 'The Short Cut'", 94-*23*
Santayana, 69
Saraswati, Satyanand, 129
Sardesai, Rajdeep, 101
Sartre, 15
Savarkar, V.D., 122-*18*
Schaeffer, Jean Marie
   "Literay Genres and Textual Generecity", 104
Scholes, Robert,
   Textual Power, 96
Scholes and Kellog, 111
   The Nature of Narrative, 111-12
Seltzer, Mark
   Henry James and the Art of Power, 93-8
Shahi Imam, 137, 138
Shakespeare, 19, 20, 28, 65

King Lear, 28
Romeo and Juliet, 39
Sharma, Ram Bilas, 150
Shepherd, Ben, 105
"Showbiz Imperialiasm: The Case of Peter Lobengula", 105
Shiv Sena, 101
Singh, Frances B., 114
"Progress and History in J.G. Farrell's *The Siege of Krishnapur*", 114, 115
Singh, Madho, 120
Singh, Man, 120, 121
Singh, V.P., 135, 137, 138
Smith, Shiela
The Other Nation, 60-61-4
Spenser, 35
Spurling, John, 113
"As Does the Bishop", 113, 115
Stalin, 151
Stang, Richard
The Theory of the Novel in England (1850-1870), 61-62-29
Steel, Flora Annie, 118
On the Face of the Waters, 118
Stephen, Fitz James, 56
"The License of Modern Novelists", 56
Stone, William B.
Idiolect and Ideology: Some Stylistic Aspects of Norris, James, Dubois", 93-15
Sun Yat Sen, 147

Tagore, 20, 129, 150
Taine, Hippolyte
Notes on England, 61-15
Thackeray, W.M., 65

Thackerey, Bal, 101
Trollope, 65
The Daily Mail, 105
The Spectator, 105
The Times of India, 101
Tolstoy, 20

Upadhyaya, Din Dayal, 138

Vishwanathan, Gauri, 37
Masks of Conquests, 37, 40-2, 4

Wallerstein, 131, 145
Walters, Margaret, 85
The Awkward Age, 85
Westminster Review, 55, 56, 62-30
White, Allon, 89
The Uses of Obscurity, 89, 93-18
White, Hayden, 112
"The Value of Narrative in the Representation of Reality", 112
Whitman, 20
Williams, Raymond, 9, 69, 70, 73, 74,
Culture and Society, 70
"Dickens and Social Ideas", 70, 74
Marxism and Literature, 9
The English Novel from Dickens to Lawrence, 69, 73, 93-19
Wilson, Edmund, 69
Wohl, S. Anthony, 49-50
The Eternal Slum, 49-50
Wordsworth, 19

Yeazell, Ruth B., 86
Language and Knowledge in the Late Novels of Henry James, 86-87, 92-7
York Notes, 109-10